THE BOOK THAT TEACHES LEADERSHIP THROUGH DIFFICULT, FUN, AND ADVENTUROUS STORIES... JUST LIKE ATTENDING WEST POINT

Let's be honest. Many leadership books can be dry. Instead of reading another repetitive book, search no more for a captivating guide. In "The Diary of a West Point Cadet," by Captain Preston Pysh, the author teaches essential West Point leadership through the most fun and unique reading of any book in its class. If you are an aspiring cadet, a small-group leader, or even an emerging leader in corporate America, this book is for you. Each intriguing firsthand account of Preston's most memorable stories from attending West Point will capture your interest and imagination. At the conclusion of each gripping story, Preston efficiently summarizes how the experience taught him lessons about leadership, which later prepared him to be a combat commander. If you like twists and turns while reading and learning, you are in for a treat. Prepare to be glued to your seat and the text as you experience unforgettable stories and lessons from "The Point."

The Diary of a
West Point Cadet

Preston Pysh
Class of 2003

Library of Congress Cataloging-in-Publication Data

Pysh, Preston G.
    The Diary of a West Point Cadet/Preston Pysh
      p. cm.
    ISBN 978-0-9829676-0-7
    1. Leadership
    2. Military - Leadership
    3. Military - History

This publication is designed to provide accurate and authoritative information in regard to the subject matter covered. It is sold with the understanding that neither the author nor the publisher is registered experts in the subject matter discussed. If legal advice or other expert assistance is required, the services of a competent professional person should be sought.

PYLON PUBLISHING

Attention: Schools and Businesses

www.pylonpublishing.com

Pylon Publishing books are available at quantity discounts with bulk purchase for educational, business, or sales promotional use. For information go to www.pylonpublishing.com

Contents

R Day

Earl Mowery, Nancy Mowery (gandparents), Gwen Pysh
(mother), and me. My dad was taking the photo.

1

The Beast

Ilooked down the long line of 18-year-old women and men who were ready to enter Michie Stadium. Everyone was accompanied by as many family members that were interested in attending. Since the gates to the stadium were not open yet, I found myself curiously looking around. I was wearing a short-sleeved T-shirt and shorts, and by the looks of everyone else, they were dressed just as casual. I was only allowed to bring one small bag, so I carried just the essentials: toothpaste, deodorant, a change of underwear, and one small picture frame that I had turned into a collage of photos. Looking down the line of my future classmates, most looked athletic and ready for the challenge. I was really excited because I had worked so hard to get accepted, yet at the same time I was apprehensive, for obvious reasons. As I stood daydreaming at the entrance to the stadium, I began to reflect on my journey to enter the Long Gray Line.

I thought about the small farm town I came from, called Saxonburg, Pennsylvania. The town's population of 2,000 provided a nice, sheltered life for a young adult. At the beginning of my 10th-grade year in high school, my family paid a visit to a close relative who worked at West Point in New York. For me, it was just another trip to visit our enormous family, but after the stay, I was captivated. I viewed a school full of students who were actively involved in sports and extracurricular activities, which far exceeded anything I had ever seen. For example, my cousin, Colonel John McLaughlin, who my family was visiting that weekend, was the coach of the West Point fencing team. I had the unique opportunity during my visit to attend practice and meet his team. I was so impressed with the manners and aptitude of the students he coached that I wanted to emulate their demeanor. I looked at the way the students treated Colonel McLaughlin, and I wanted to be him. At such a young age, I had never looked at personnel in the military with much admiration. My lack of respect wasn't because I disliked the service, but because I was never really exposed to it. This perception drastically changed after my weekend visiting my relatives. I viewed the military, and West Point, as an institution that was bigger than myself. I desperately wanted to be part of this organization.

At the time of my visit, my grades in high school were marginal. My grandfather and dad always believed I was capable of getting accepted into the Academy, but they also assured me it wouldn't be easy. They were adamant that my current academic standing would not make me competitive for admission, but they also encouraged me to chase my dreams. Hearing this and seeing what I wanted, I had no choice but to conduct a complete role reversal of the student I was. Like any goal, the start was difficult. I studied harder than I ever had in my entire life. I was a "B" student who occasionally got "C's," so the transformation was going to be laborious and most likely gradual. My parents could tell I was truly inspired by the trip to West Point. Instead of coming home from school and watching TV, I would go directly to my room to start studying. When my mom caught me waking up early to get extra studying in before tests, she obviously knew a drastic transformation was underway.

At the end of my first grading period that year, I came home to tell my mom that I had received straight "A's" on my report card. I remember the look she gave me when I told her the great news.

She said, "OK, let's see your report card." A little hesitant, I replied, "I haven't got it yet." "Oh. Well, when you get it, I'd love to see it," she said in return.

I can still remember the slight doubt in her voice when she talked to me that afternoon, because I had never received straight "A's" in my entire life.

The next morning when I went to class, I remember looking at my desk when I entered the room and seeing all the report cards flipped upside down on everyone's desks. As I timidly approached my table, I made a last-second dash and quickly flipped over the page like I was ripping off a Band-aid to avoid the pain. Looking down the list of classes that semester, I realized my poor academic performance in the past was purely induced by a lack of effort as opposed to a lack of talent. I had just received straight "A's" for the first time in my life.

As the year progressed, I continued to excel due to hard work and dedication. In fact, by my junior year, I was taking advanced placement classes. I was working harder than ever to accomplish my absolute desire to attend West Point. As the semesters flew by, I achieved my goal of conducting the academic role reversal I had sought. Toward the end of my senior year, I received a large packet in the mail from West Point's director of admissions. I felt a large folder was a better indication than a small letter-sized envelope. As I opened the packet with as much enthusiasm as I had when flipping over my report card three years earlier, I realized I had accomplished my goal. I was accepted and manifested for summer training. I only had one month after high school graduation to report to what everyone referred to as "Beast Barrack." It didn't sound very inviting, but I had no choice. I couldn't become a West Point cadet without first completing "Beast."

As I continued to contemplate my high school journey, I was startled by the loud and authoritative voice of a cadet standing at the entrance to the stadium.

"Everyone secure your gear and move to the seats inside the stadium. Please fill the seats from the front to the back."

It was time. My family and I moved through the gates and into the stadium in order to sit along the 50-yard line. After everyone filled the seats, an officer dressed in his green uniform started to talk to all the future students and their family members. I really wasn't paying attention to what he was saying because I was more concerned about leaving my family behind. The officer's babbling didn't last long, but the last sentence struck a chord with everyone sitting in the stadium.

"You have two minutes to say goodbye to your families. At the end of the two minutes, all cadet candidates need to be lined up in the center aisle of the stadium."

I really don't remember what I said to my parents that day, but I remember being strong despite the terrible feeling in my stomach. I was one of those kids who was truly blessed to have the best parents and grandparents in the entire world. When given only two minutes to say goodbye, it almost felt like a slap in the face for everything they had done to help me achieve my goal. Regardless of my feelings, I stayed strong and found myself standing in the center aisle with the rest of my new classmates in only a moment's notice.

After everyone was assembled, one cadet, dressed in his white-over-gray uniform, walked to the lead candidate and escorted us across the 50-yard line. As we walked across the football field, I could hear the crowd of parents remaining in the stands begin clapping for us. I looked back as I continued moving forward to hopefully catch a glimpse of my family one last time. As I sustained my visual search, I had already walked to the other side of the field and was getting ready to enter a tunnel that was used for the opposing football team's locker room. As I rounded the corner into the tunnel, our proud line of cadet candidates was instantly whipped into submission. The moment we were out of our parents' field of view, the real West Point experience began.

"What in the world are you looking around for?" One sizeable upperclassman said to me as I passed by his position. "All of you. STOP LOOKING AROUND!" This time he wasn't talking authoritatively; he was screaming.

I had only been yelled at like that a few times in my entire life, and within the first five seconds of being with these upperclassmen, they were sending a message that instructions would only be given once. As we continued to file into the locker room, all my lackadaisical classmates were quickly transformed into robots that showed no emotion, made no noise, and remained motionless. We were directed to fill out forms and stand in certain spots on the floor. As we were filling out the paperwork, I heard a guy a few rows down ask a question.

"Sir, my parents recently moved this week. Should I list the old address or the new one?"

The upperclassman standing right next to the guy shouted back so fast he could have continued his sentence.

"YOU CAN'T BE SERIOUS! I'll tell you what. List your old address. That way when you quit next week, we'll mail that fruity bag you're holding to the wrong place."

I couldn't see what was happening because I was too afraid to look left, but evidently my classmate's emotions hadn't been flushed out of his system yet. After hearing the upperclassman's response, my classmate evidently rolled his eyes and continued writing on the piece of paper. As he continued writing, I could tell that the upperclassman swiftly moved right in front of the table where the eye-roller was standing.

Since the room was completely silent, I could hear

the upperclassman quietly say, "Is there something you didn't like about my response?"

Nothing was said; my eye-rolling classmate was absolutely mute. Then in a sudden rampage, the upperclassman reversed his polite questions and began to scream.

"DID YOU NOT LIKE MY RESPONSE? I swear to God and everyone in this room, I'm going to personally devote every ounce of my efforts this summer 'developing' just you."

I could hear the upperclassman rip the piece of paper from under my classmate's hand and continue to speak while looking at the page.

"Perez. Your name is Perez. All right, Pee-rez, I got your number."

Silence instantly filled the room after the upperclassman finished. It was like someone had pulled the plug on an obnoxious radio that was blaring out of control. Needless to say, I kept my mouth shut and just tried to look like the next guy. Before arriving, I had anticipated the hazing and mind games as somewhat droll, but the intensity in this room was nothing like I had imagined. What in the world was I getting myself into? This was my first five minutes at West Point; I only had four years to go.

The reception day, or R-Day, was one of the most disorienting experiences of my life. It's a day I'll never forget, yet vaguely remember. I had never forced my body to remain so still and move so little. As a result, I experienced cramps in my body that I didn't even know could exist. I felt like a chess piece that was strategically being moved from station to station with precise timing and purpose at all times. I didn't know why I was moving to a new area or why I was standing at parade rest for thirty minutes. I just did. Not being able to look around or speak put me in a world I had never experienced. I had relinquished reasoning and independence and placed them before the stony gates of the institution. By releasing these instinctual characteristics, I was essentially allowing someone else to control my purpose.

Rules and regulations were being demanded of us after each and every move. The amount of information that we were required to memorize was like trying to drink water from a fire hose. At each station, there were new instructions and new requirements. Anytime someone wasn't paying attention or did anything outside the guidance of the upperclassmen, they were instantly reprimanded harshly. I distinctly remember how we were expected to know the standards before even being taught the regulations. My whole life, I had only dealt with teachers and leaders who allowed an amnesty period when new ideas and concepts were established. West Point was different; amnesty didn't exist. The upperclassmen expected us to know all the rules and regulations upon arrival. As a result of us obviously not knowing all the standards, there was a lot of yelling, and discipline was implemented immediately.

As R-Day progressed, I realized it was organized as a system of stations. There were upperclassmen assigned to each station, and we were the pawns that needed to get signed off at each location. One of the first stations was getting us into uniform. After the first location, we had to wear tags on our hip so the upperclassmen could sign us off for each station we completed. Essentially, we were like tagged cattle in order for the upper class to keep accountability of each location we attended. By mid-afternoon, I had all my uniforms, a new room, a bald head, a medical examination, classes on marching and other military courtesies, and numerous other areas that all seemed like a blur.

It was about 4:00 p.m. when I was instructed to get in my room and change into a white-over-gray uniform like the one I saw the upperclassmen wearing. For the first time that day, the upperclassmen seemed to be in a rush. They weren't taking a lot of time to make corrections and yell; they were just trying to make sure we got in our uniforms as fast as possible. I ran into my new room and put on the uniform as best as I could. I really didn't know how everything was supposed to go, so I just tried to make it look like their's. I was instructed to get changed, then open my door and stand at the entrance. As I waited patiently by my door, I quickly glanced in the mirror and couldn't believe my eyes. I could barely recognize myself. *Wow, I look terrible with a bald head*, I thought to myself. As I was looking in the mirror, an upperclassman walked past my room. He scooped me up with all the other new cadets who were following his lead. As the upperclassman ran up and down the long hall looking for more new cadets, he quickly came back to the spot where he left us. There were about ten of us standing at attention along the side of the hall.

Looking at and talking to us like we were 5 years old, he said, "OK, new cadets. Do you think you can walk down three flights of steps to the first floor without me?"

We all looked at him and didn't say anything. At this point in the day, everyone was afraid to stand out. As a result, we all just listened and didn't respond.

With a sense of urgency in his voice, the upperclassman continued, "OK, I need you to go to the end of the hall and go down the steps. Once you get to the bottom of the steps you will find someone to assist you. I have to stay here and get more of you slowpokes."

After he was done talking, I saw one member of our group start to turn toward the stairwell. As a result of his lead, everyone else followed. We scurried down the hall and then the steps only to find ourselves walking out of the large stone building and into a sally port. Once the ten of us got outside, we heard a drum and saw hundreds of our classmates in a large open area marching in circles. We didn't know where to go after we got outside, so we just stood there.

We didn't talk to each other or move; we just stood there like cattle that were prepared to get slaughtered. In only a couple hours of being at the Academy, our minds had been so warped that we didn't have an ounce of independence left to make decisions. As we remained in the same location, we saw one upperclassman speed walk toward our position. He started talking to us as he continued his approach.

"What company are you in?"

All ten of our sets of eyes started shifting left and right because we weren't allowed to turn our heads. No one knew the answer to his question. I thought to myself, "What the hell is a company?"

As the upperclassman got closer, he asked a little louder, "What company are you new cadets in?"

Again, not one of us responded. I could tell the upperclassman was frustrated. He would have gotten a better response out of a 4 year old at this point. His irritation stemmed from the fact we weren't wearing our "cattle tags" because we had changed uniforms. As a result, he couldn't identify which company we were supposed to be with.

The upperclassman was scrambling for ideas when his expression changed and he quickly questioned, "What floor did you guys just come from in that building?"

Everyone remained silent.

Getting more angry, the upperclassman questioned again, "What floor did you just get changed on?"

As I stood there silent, I heard one of my classmates reply, "The third floor, Sir."

Without any hesitation, he said, "Great. Bravo Company. Follow me, cadidiots."

Before he even finished his comment, he was already

darting away.

As we followed the large upperclassman through the crowd of cadets marching in a confined area, I realized all these people were my classmates. There were over a thousand people in this small area and they were all marching in formation. It literally looked like a maze of patterned people and yet the upperclassman knew exactly where to take us just by knowing what floor we changed our clothes on.

As we approached a formation of about 100 cadets, we heard the escorting upperclassman shout, "Bravo, these are some of yours."

After hearing the escort's announcement, I saw an upperclassman in the front of the formation raise his hand and yell back, "Thanks, we got 'em."

At this point, we stopped following the upperclassman who brought us to the location and two new upperclassmen gathered us up. They immediately started shouting out our last names as they read our name tapes that hung on our right breast pocket. As they called out each of our names, we would hear a corresponding shout from the large formation.

When they called my name, I heard a holler come from the front of the formation, "Send him here."

As I approached a moderately built upper-class male, he got in my face.

He said, "Pysh, you're in first squad, first platoon, Bravo Company. You can't forget that! Now get in formation."

With a confused look on my face, I replied, "Sir, what information do you want me to get?"

Pausing for a brief second to think about my question, I could tell he didn't have a response.

Trying not to laugh, the upperclassman replied, "Pysh, I said get-in-the-formation, not get information."

Luckily, my stupidity was funny enough to make the

upperclassman break the stern image he was trying to project. As a result, he just let me leave and stand next to the hundred other people who were directly behind the spot where we just conversed. As I got into position, I saw that same upperclassman walk over to one of his comrades and whisper something in his ear. At the end of their conversation, they both started laughing and looking back at me. I knew they were talking about my idiotic comment. This was so humiliating. I had never felt so small and dumb. This was a feeling I became very familiar with that summer.

As I stood at parade rest, my hands were held together behind my back and my feet were shoulder-width apart. I heard one of the upperclassmen begin talking to everyone in the formation.

"Listen up, new cadets."

As all our little eyes focused on the man speaking, he slowly took off his white hat.

"You're going to wear this hat until the day you graduate. You need to take great pride in wearing this piece of uniform. I can just look at cadets who wear their hats and tell if they're going to make it. As you can see, there is a shiny little crest in the middle that you're responsible for shining every day. If you have any pride, you'll file the lines out of the flag so you can get it even brighter. This takes a lot of work and determination, just like making it through this institution. So before you go to bed tonight, shine the brass on your hats."

As the upperclassman walked away, everyone stored that piece of information away with the 10 trillion other things we had already been told.

Although it didn't seem like there was any point to all the formations and marching, we were actually being prepped for a parade. After thirty minutes of marching and practicing commands in the area around the barracks, I heard a band begin to play. As soon as the music started, we continued our rehearsal out of a sally port at the base of the barracks. Not very far past the buildings, we found ourselves in line and marching down a road that was lined with people watching and taking photos. I knew there was a method to all the detailed directions that day, but even I had to admit, it was incredible knowing what the upperclassmen had done. They had assembled us all into a parade without us even realizing what was happening.

After marching down the road to an area called Trophy Point, the band stopped playing and the upperclassmen started barking orders. We were executing right and left faces like we had been practicing earlier in the day at one of the stations. As we turned toward the Hudson River, I could get a good look at all the people who were lining the street for the parade. After my entire class had executed a left face, I heard a bunch of people start talking over an intercom system. We were in a parade and in front of all our families because we were taking an oath to serve the U.S. Army and the Constitution of the United States. As we said the oath, chills ran down my back because I knew I was now a part of that organization that was bigger than myself. The ceremony only lasted a few minutes before everyone was ordered back into marching formation. During the entire event, we never broke ranks and never spoke to anyone lining the streets. We remained completely silent and obeyed the orders being shouted by the upperclassmen. While marching back toward the barracks, our formations were redirected toward the mess hall.

Once we got close to the steps of the massive hall, we were ordered to fall out and put our right hands on the shoulders of the personnel in front of our position. Although I didn't realize the purpose at the time, this was a way for the upperclassman to keep accountability of all their squads. This was a difficult task, considering 1,200 new cadets entered the large doors of the mess hall all at the same time. I felt like I was back in first grade, being led down the hall to art class by my teacher. After making our way through the maze of tables, we finally arrived at our dining area. The upperclassmen who led us to that location ordered us to find a seat and stand at parade rest. As we waited for everyone to get to their tables, which took less than five minutes, I heard an announcement.

"Regiment, attention."

After everyone in the massive room came to attention, we were ordered to take our seats all at the same time. As I sat down with my nine new cadet classmates, the one upperclassman at the table started barking all kinds of orders.

He looked right at me and said, "Pysh, you need to announce the drink for the meal."

Not knowing what to say, I looked back at the upperclassman and said, "Sir, the drink is Kool-Aid."

Furious, he pounded his fist on the table and said, "New Cadet Pysh, you will hold the pitcher of fruit punch over your right shoulder and announce the drink like this."

Unconventionally, the upperclassman reached across the table and grabbed the pitcher of punch to demonstrate the procedure.

"Once you get the pitcher like this, you'll make the following announcement: Sir, the cold beverage for this meal is fruit punch. Does anyone not care for fruit punch, Sir?"

After making the announcement at lightening speed, he slammed the pitcher back on the table and told the other new cadets to pass it down to where I was sitting.

"Now you try," the upperclassman exclaimed.

As I got my hands on the pitcher, I slowly lifted it over my right shoulder and started the announcement.

"Sir, the drink for this..."

"Stop, just stop. It's not a drink, it's a cold beverage. You don't pay attention to details, Pysh," the upperclassman shouted at me. "Do it again."

As I slowly lifted the pitcher over my shoulder again, I timidly started the announcement.

"Sir, the cold beverage is fruit punch..."

As if cutting my sentence in half with a knife, the upperclassman sharply interrupted again.

"For this meal! You said, 'The cold beverage is fruit punch.' The correct format is 'The cold beverage for this meal is fruit punch.' I don't know if you're just slow or you're from Texas, but you better start listening really fast or it's going to be a long year, Pysh. Can anyone at the table announce the cold beverage?"

As soon as the upperclassman finished his sentence, one of my classmates suggested that he could complete the task.

When I passed the pitcher down the table to the volunteer, he held it over his shoulder and said, "Sir, the cold beverage for this meal is fruit punch. Does anyone not care for fruit punch?"

As the volunteer continued to hold the beverage above his right shoulder, the upperclassman continued to look at him like he wasn't done. The volunteer could tell that there was something missing. The utter silence at the table was so frustrating because no one could tell what this demanding upperclassman wanted. All we knew was that we just experienced one of the most draining days of our lives and we just wanted something to drink, let alone eat. As we watched and waited, the upperclassman broke the silence.

"SIR! You need to finish the second sentence with 'sir.' Anytime you say two sentences, you better put two 'sirs' on them." After a brief pause he continued. "Just pour the drinks. I can't take your stupidity any longer."

Evidently, we were supposed to announce all the

dishes at the table in a similar format. As a result of our failure to announce the cold beverage in a timely manner, he made us eat in the five minutes that remained for the meal.

Later that evening, I was sent back to my room to start preparing for the next day. It was about 9 o'clock at night when I finally closed the door to the chaos in the halls. As I walked into my room, I met my roommate for the first time. Initially, we just looked at each other like, "Holy hell, we can finally talk and be normal." The short pause and look was actually quite funny because we were obviously thinking the same thing. He introduced himself as Scott Montoya from Albuquerque, New Mexico, while I introduced myself as a Steelers fan from Pittsburgh, Pennsylvania. It was such a relief to finally talk to someone without getting screamed at. That night, Scott and I chatted about everything we had endured throughout the day. We both agreed it was infinitely harder than we had expected.

At 10:00 p.m., Scott and I heard a bugler play Taps. We assumed someone was going to come by our room and make sure we were still there. We didn't know if it would be better to be in bed or get caught studying "knowledge" at our desks. With only a short amount of time to decide, we both decided to get caught in the room studying instead of sleeping. We could hear some knocking at doors down the hall, so we were only moments away from finding out the right answer. Before our room was checked, Scott and I agreed to sleep on top of the covers to save time in the morning. We were instructed earlier in the day on the complex procedure for making a tight bed and wanted to avoid the long procedure if at all possible. As we concluded our conversation, there were two loud and thunderous knocks at our door. Before we could even respond, the door flew open and an upperclassman instantly corrected our decision to study behind our desk.

"What are you two doing out of bed? As soon as you hear Taps, you need to be in your beds. Now get there."

After hearing the upperclassman's demands, we jumped out of our seats and carefully climbed on top of our bunks, not breaking the covers. As we lay on our backs, the upperclassman identified our ploy. He could see we were lying on our beds like they were made of thin ice. Watching our subtle movements, the upperclassman commented further.

"Walk-up is at 0430 in order to get ready for 0500 PT (Physical Training). Do you guys want me to give you a tip for PT tomorrow?"

Excited that we were going to get an inside tip from one of the upperclassmen, Scott and I gave a resounding, "Yes, Sir!"

The upperclassman was showing a lot of excitement and sympathy for Scott and me as he began explaining his tip.

"OK, when you conduct PT tomorrow, everything is going to be done in a cadence. For example, there's this exercise called the 'flutter kick.' During that exercise, you'll lie on your back with your hands under your butts and you'll kick your legs up and down. You're not allowed to touch the ground with your feet until the leader concludes the cadence. Do you guys want to try it real quick so you're prepared for tomorrow?"

As we heard this great information, Scott and I responded with an animated, "Yes, Sir!"

The upperclassman at this point was showing just as much excitement when he said, "OK, get under your covers and I'll start the cadence."

At this point, Scott and I knew we had been duped as we slowly climbed under the covers. Once we were established under the tightly fitted sheets, the upperclassman began the cadence.

"Great, let's begin. 1, 2, 3, 4, 1, 2, 3, 4..."

After each number, Scott and I kicked the tight corners out of our bed. After about a minute, our beds looked like they had been made by kindergartners.

At the end of the exercise, the upperclassman turned off the lights and said, "Sweet dreams and welcome to West Point."

After the upperclassman left our room, Scott whispered quietly, "What a dick. Let's get up and make our beds so we won't need to in the morning. Besides, I have more stuff I want to get done. We'll just be quiet and keep the lights off."

Scott didn't even need to say anything because I was already thinking the same thing. Without responding, I slowly climbed out of my bed and helped Scott put his bunk back together. After we helped each other make the beds, I grabbed my white hat and started to file the lines out of the crest. I was heeding the upperclassman's advice on getting the brass as shiny as I could.

Scott and I worked until midnight before we decided to call it a day. After calling it quits, we delicately climbed back onto our beds and rested our heads. We slept well that night, despite the fire alarm that rang at 2:30 a.m. and got us out of bed and into formation for 30 minutes.

* * *

For the rest of the book, I'm going to refer to this portion of each chapter as the Bottom Line Up-Front, or BLUF for short. For many, the stories and events that occur in each chapter might appear to have no point or purpose. As a result, it is this section where I will detail why I think the story has significant meaning. Essentially, I'll make sense of the nonsense.

The BLUF of this story is a basic fundamental: leaders need to learn how to listen and follow orders before they can lead.

R-Day truly was a horrible experience. At the time, I couldn't understand the purpose of Beast Barracks. It seemed more like a "rite of passage" exercise than anything else. Although this was my first inclination, it was, in fact, teaching us the importance of listening and following orders.

One of the most difficult things for a person to do is listen. How many times have you approached your boss or superior and could tell he wasn't interested in hearing your opinions or ideas? You could have talked to the wall and received more feedback. Think about how frustrated you became after watching his eyes and mind totally avoid your input. This is something that leaders must always remember. Subordinates have a strong potential to provide great input. In many cases, they may know far more information than you as a leader. Sometimes, just shutting up and listening to what they have to say is more valuable than the detailed analysis provided by others. When a leader doesn't give his subordinates the appropriate respect and venue to provide their input, frustration and information sharing is inhibited from the bottom up. If subordinates perceive disrespect, their desire to continue helping the leader diminishes rapidly. In essence, this diminished information flow is the by-product of a leader's inability to listen to his subordinates. In the story, it became evident within the first couple of minutes that our input was not welcome. If we spoke, we were instantly reprimanded and marginalized. The result of this lack of listening by the upperclassmen was an immediate withdrawal of input. We were too scared to talk because we knew our ideas or thoughts would never be considered. In the story, this was a good thing. In real life and under normal managerial circumstances, this is a bad thing. The only reason I bring this point to your attention is because the upperclassmen's stubborn attitudes provided an extreme example to illustrate my point: Failing to listen will handicap a leader. Superiors need to recognize that even the smallest amount of stubborn behavior, with respect to listening to their subordinates, can negatively affect the flow of information sharing. I've always found it was never my ears that got me into trouble.

Everyone likes to be the leader because leaders make the rules. When you look at a class of young kids, everyone wants to be in charge of a game or activity. This is a common human behavior for many people. Sometimes, leaders don't emerge because they are the best people for the job. Instead, they emerge because they want the job or position more than the others. As a result, some leaders have minimal experience or lack perspective. This lack of experience inhibits this type of leader's judgment because he can never put himself in his subordinates' positions. A great example is a young adult who takes over a company that was family owned. This young leader might walk into a room where he is the supervisor of ten subordinates. As a result, he is severely handicapped because he never experienced the orders he requires of his juniors. This was the primary reason Beast Barracks and the whole first year was structured the way it was. The purpose was to give future leaders the perspective of their subordinates.

I hardly need to add that this training and perspective is something many leaders across America have lost sight of over the years. Recently, our country has seen an economic credit crisis in which millions of jobs were lost due to a lack of credible leaders and regulators. I would like to focus on the first reason: leadership. As CEOs of failed financial institutions continued to collect billions of dollars from taxpayers, many also continued to receive multimillion-dollar bonuses while their lower-income employees lost their jobs. If one CEO would have taken a million dollars less in personal bonus money, he could have saved twenty jobs, if not more. Some of these greedy

CEOs lost or never even had the perspective of their subordinates. Looking at this situation alone, one can clearly see why understanding the perspectives of your subordinates is essential. West Point firmly educates its cadets that learning to follow before you can lead is the foundation of any leader. Maybe some of these "leaders" on Wall Street should have taken a closer look at a leader like Dwight D. Eisenhower who said, "Humility must always be the portion of any man who receives acclaim earned in the blood of his followers and the sacrifices of his friends."

2

Deliveries, Duties, and Dismay

It was the last week of Beast Barracks and anticipation was running high. I had almost completed the hardest summer of my entire life. The training was coming to a close and I was trying to prepare myself for the dreaded academic year, which I heard was mentally abusive. Rumors among my friends were that the classes at West Point were going to be extremely difficult compared to anything we had experienced in high school. We were worried, to say the least. Despite the fear of the demanding academics, there was something else that was even more dreadful: the additional upperclassmen. During Beast Barracks, there were about nine new cadets for every one upperclassman. This ratio was already very difficult to become accustomed to. I knew at the end of Beast, 3,000 upperclassmen would drastically change the ratio of new cadets to upperclassmen.

During the last week of Beast, I could see new cadets become even more depressed with the anticipation of the change that was upon us. The new leadership and the increase in upperclassmen was going to radically affect the way we conducted business around the campus. In an effort to get the new cadets away from the university while the upperclassmen returned, we hiked fifteen miles into the woods to live for a week. This allowed the returning upperclassmen to set up their rooms while we finalized our last days of training for the summer. For the last week, we learned numerous weapons and combat skills while living in the wilderness.

Back at the school, all the upperclassmen began returning from the various summer details to which they had been assigned. The Firsties (seniors) and Cows (juniors) had specialized training in which they had the opportunity to attended things like air assault training or complete internships with governmental organizations. They could even get a job working with the Central Intelligence Agency (CIA) or the National Aeronautical and Space Administration (NASA). As a new cadet at the Academy, this kind of training sounded much more interesting than the summer I was currently experiencing. The instruction for them was definitely tailored toward their personal desires. I figured these luxuries would come as I paid my dues.

The Yearlings (sophomores), on the other hand, were returning from a summer of training at Camp Buckner. This is a camp that's about seven miles away from the West Point campus where cadets learn the majority of their military skills. For the whole second summer, the Yearlings focused on all the different weapon systems the Army has at its disposal. They get the chance to fire anti-tank rocket launchers, fully automatic machine guns, drive and shoot Abrams tanks, and shoot artillery rounds. Cadets currently attending the Academy refer to Camp Buckner as Camp Buckistan or Buckraq, but the old graduates always call it Bucknam. At the end of their training, the Yearlings would run seven miles back to the campus as motivation to start the new academic year.

The last group of cadets to return for the summer were the new cadets from Beast Barracks. The night before our return to garrison, we prepared our legs and minds for the fifteen-mile journey that was upon us. We were worried because we knew there was going to be little sympathy from the thousands of upperclassmen back in the barracks. We heard rumors from our cadre that most of the upperclassmen were very anxious to get their hands on us. The morning of our return, Scott and I packed all our belongings into our large backpacks and started the long hike back to the Academy. It was really early and the moon was still out when we started. It was a painful journey, and many of the guys still had blood blisters on their feet from the trudge out there. The heat was extremely intense, and the long-sleeved shirts and pants tucked into our boots sure didn't help alleviate the agonizing distance. As we completed the 15-mile excursion at approximately 1200 o'clock in the afternoon, the college campus appeared to be very quiet. Despite our excitement to arrive and get showers and warm meals, it was profoundly overshadowed by our fear of the additional upperclassmen. To our surprise, as we marched the final steps back to the apron of the parade field, there were no signs of additional upperclassmen present.

As we grounded our gear, the cadre in charge of Beast said, "OK, everyone form up. We're gettin' some food."

This was like music to our ears. We quickly grounded our gear and hobbled into formation. My feet felt like I had scrubbed them with sandpaper the whole morning. As we walked into the mess hall, which was usually empty, we quickly realized things were going to be different. As I entered the massive hall with an expectation of seeing a bunch of empty seats, I saw the enormous building was already housing 3,000 upper-class cadets. I couldn't believe my eyes. This was even scarier than I had expected. As we slowly entered the mess, I began passing thousands of men and women who were clearly excited to see our return.

I could hear them yelling, "Look, it's the new cadets. They look like they just finished making brownies all summer."

As we sat down in our seats, I could sense the 3,000

sets of eyes staring laser beams through our heads. I knew this wasn't going to be a good day. It was lunchtime and I had already hiked fifteen miles with a sixty-pound backpack, and now I was going to put up with all these salivating upperclassmen.

At the conclusion of the meal, we were sent to our new companies. During Beast Barracks, there were 8 companies comprised of 90 percent new cadets. Now, the roles were reversed and we were being reorganized into 32 companies that were made up of 75 percent upperclassmen. A lot of my close friends from the summer were being sent to different companies and I would need to start meeting new classmates all over again. After being marched to my new company area, I could hear and see upperclassmen everywhere. As we stood in front of our new dorms, or barracks, I could hear people screaming and yelling from inside the buildings. It sounded like absolute chaos.

The new upperclassman now running our formation shouted, "All right, ground all your gear and line up in a single-file line by last name."

After he made the announcement, we began slowly putting our heavy bags on the ground, as our backs and legs were extremely sore. As most new cadets had half their gear on the ground, the upperclassman furiously barked a new set of orders.

"Evidently you didn't like that request. When I speak you move. I don't tolerate slow movement and little motivation. Evidently you didn't want to put those heavy bags on the ground, so you can just continue wearing them for the rest of the day."

Hearing the new request, we couldn't believe our ears. This guy couldn't be serious. As we began putting all the heavy bags and equipment back on our shoulders, about fifteen more upperclassmen surrounded our small formation of new cadets. It was like they were coming out of the woodwork. A couple of them, anxious to get their hands on the new freshmen, infiltrated the formation and started getting in people's faces.

I heard the one upperclassman say, "Do you really think we weren't watching you from inside the building? We could clearly see your lack of motivation and effort. If you want to be part of Company G1, then you better start acting like you want to fit in."

As he finished, another upperclassman began, "Hey, I have a good idea. Why don't we do some push-ups? Maybe that might motivate them."

The leader, again taking charge, said, "That sounds like a great idea." As he called the formation to attention, he began barking strict orders. "Platoon, half right...face. Front leaning rest position...move."

This was the specific command they would use to get us in the push-up position. As we held our bodies and our sixty-pound backpacks off the ground with just our arms, we anxiously awaited the upperclassman's command to begin.

Taking at least a minute before speaking, the upperclassman said, "All right, I don't want to make things too hard for you guys, so we'll just do twenty push-ups. You will only go down when I say down and you will only go up when I say up. Do you understand?"

With my arms already completely exhausted from waiting to start the exercise, I responded back in unison with my classmates, "Yes, Sergeant."

As the upperclassman started giving the command to go up and down, it was clear that doing twenty push-ups was going to be equivalent to doing sixty or more. He was calling the cadence slower than anything I had heard all summer. If there was an event that was symbolic for the rest of the week, it would have been those push-ups. The reorganization week was extremely long, painful, and arduous.

As new plebes (freshmen) in an academic company, we had numerous duties outside of the standard academics. Three of the most painful extra duties were calling minutes, picking up trash, and laundry. Since the plebes were organized into three platoons for each company, the three major duties would rotate between platoons each week. Even though a specific platoon was assigned a duty, all the plebes would usually help each other complete the tasks.

Calling minutes was a duty that required the plebes in a company to essentially be alarm clocks for the upperclassmen. Before each major event throughout the day, plebes would line up in front of all the clocks in the barracks and count down the minutes before each formation. Plebes would call minutes for breakfast, lunch, dinner, drill, class meetings, and anything else that involved notification of a major event. Learning this duty at the beginning was very painful. Imagine a long hallway with four or five clocks every hundred feet. Under each clock stood one plebe who was ready to shout as loud as he could. Exactly eight minutes before the actual formation or event, all the plebes would start the loud and obnoxious announcement.

We would yell, "Attention all cadets. There are five minutes until assembly for dinner formation. The uniform is full dress. Five minutes remaining."

Although that seems short and to the point, that simple announcement would typically take about thirty seconds to say. We would start the announcement three minutes early to allow more time for the upperclassmen to get to their destination. It was by their request, so we just executed and didn't ask questions. The upperclassmen normally wouldn't say anything just as long as we did four things: We had to be really loud, we had to always be on time, we weren't allowed to mess up the announcement, and most importantly, we had to make the announcement in unison. The last requirement was the one that was extremely hard. As a result of being so loud, we typically couldn't hear the other plebes making the announcement at the same time. It almost seemed impossible to keep the minute-calling in unison. For weeks, we couldn't figure out a way to scream and listen at the same time. Unfortunately for us, every time we made this mistake, it was like calling bloodhounds to the hall. Desperate to find a solution to the problem, we tried to think of a fix. Every time we tried to solve the problem, we found ourselves arguing and blaming each other instead of developing a solution; we obviously did this behind closed doors. It was hard working with each other because everyone was getting in trouble and everyone was quick to place blame.

As time progressed, one of my friends decided to start holding meetings in his room before it was time to call the minutes so we could fix the problem. Scatterbrained, we couldn't figure out a way to get the obnoxious screaming in unison. As all forty of us packed into his small room, my classmates started arguing right away. As the uproar began to get more obnoxious, one of my classmates spoke up.

"Listen, everyone. Quiet down and stop blaming each other. As stupid as this might sound, we probably need to quietly practice the announcement here, before we do it for real in the hall."

Although many didn't like the idea, they agreed it was probably necessary.

He continued, "We need to break this thing down into smaller segments that have four or five smaller parts. If we do that, we can stay in unison if no one proceeds to the next segment until they hear everyone's finished."

As he started demonstrating the idea, it started making a lot of sense to everyone. Excited about the new concept, everyone scurried to their positions in front of the numerous clocks that were throughout the hall. As we started calling the minutes in unison that day, the upper class knew we had figured out the trick.

As I stood beneath the clock calling minutes, one upperclassman passed me and said, "Wow, look. The plebes finally figured it out. It took you long enough."

The trash detail was the easiest of the three duties. Since it needed to be completed very early in the morning, most upperclassmen were not awake and willing to check on the status of the requirement. Obviously, if the duty wasn't completed, then concerns were brought to our attention.

We would sometimes play childish games because we could avoid getting in trouble. For example, when cleaning the trash out of the bathroom, we would continually flip upperclassmen's name tapes upside down on their lockers. They would often think it was their roommates or friends and never suspected us of doing such a thing. It was the little things that kept us happy.

Another little trick we conducted was slamming doors. Since it was really early in the morning and we knew all the upperclassmen were trying to sleep, we would slam doors to disrupt their sleep. The abrupt noise would wake them up, but they would never know which room caused the ruckus.

One morning, after I finished taking out the trash, I avoided a really ugly situation. It all started when I ran up the steps to get back to my room and start memorizing the required knowledge for the day. As I got to what I thought was the fourth floor, I sprinted down the hall and stopped at the entrance to my supposed room. It was very early in the morning and there was no one awake except for plebes. I tried to pull a stunt that would kill two birds with one stone: scare the hell out of my roommates and wake up every upperclassman in our hall. To prep the door, I gently turned the handle to unlatch the entrance. Once the door was slightly cracked, I took a couple steps back in order to gain some momentum. The doors were heavy duty and could really withstand a good lick. As I got a running start at the door, I jumped in the air and kicked it wide open. As the door flung open and smashed off the doorstop in an abrupt and violent manner, I knew the situation wasn't going to be good.

For starters, all the lights were off and there were only two beds in the room. As soon as the door made the loud boom, the two cadets sleeping in their beds were startled awake. Luckily, the door was kicked open so hard that it actually came off the doorstop and returned to the closed position. In the brief period the door was open, I saw the sheer terror on the faces of the upperclassmen as they were shocked awake. As the door closed right in front of my face, I read the number 304 written on the door. Realizing that my room number was 404, the whole incident became frighteningly realistic. I was now faced with a choice: continue standing at the door and await the monumental punishment or take the gamble and hope the two sleepy-eyed upperclassmen didn't notice my identity.

After contemplating my choices for under a second, I chose the latter and raced toward the stairs like an Olympic 100-meter sprinter. As I got to the stairwell undetected, I couldn't even believe the decision I just made. Throughout the rest of the day, I was on edge worrying about the potential of being caught for my actions earlier that morning. Luckily, the upperclassmen never figured out who jump-kicked their door that morning. I obviously told my roommates the incident wasn't an accident. I bragged about how daring I was in an effort to boost morale among my fellow plebes.

The third and most annoying duty was delivering laundry to all the upperclassmen. This had to be one of the worst jobs a plebe had to endure. Due to the number of students and workload, laundry is sent out to a contracted company to be cleaned. The problem occurs when the company returns the laundry in a shrink-wrapped bundle and it all needs to be sorted. The returned laundry comes in large bins that would be placed beneath the mess hall. Three times a week, the plebes would go to the basement and find their company's laundry containers and pull them back to the barracks. Once the large bins get pulled back to one of the plebe rooms, all the laundry is sorted by rank and in alphabetical order. Although seniors and juniors are the same year group, they have an entirely different rank structure, further complicating the whole ordeal.

Once the laundry was sorted, all the plebes would assemble themselves in the room and begin delivering. There are two main reasons this job was so difficult. First, laundry could not be delivered out of rank order. This posed a problem because some upperclassmen would keep you in their room in order to delay your return. The idea was that all members of the plebe class were always accountable for their peers. As a result, if one plebe got stuck in someone's room for twenty minutes, all the plebes would just wait in the room for his return before more laundry was sent out the door. The second quandary was numerous upperclassmen would wait outside the room where the laundry operation was being conducted. We used to hate these guys. We could never figure out why they didn't have something more important to do with their time than stand outside the room and make our lives miserable. As soon as someone would walk out the door with a bundle of laundry, the few upperclassmen who practically guarded the door would tell us to stop and stand by the wall. They would ask us knowledge and check our uniforms.

In actuality, it didn't help our appearance or knowledge; it just slowed us down tremendously. As the months progressed, laundry duty would literally take two hours, every other night. We began to get desperate. We would constantly argue behind closed doors, which would spark the upperclassmen standing outside the guarded laundry room to slow down operations even further. They would hear us arguing and abruptly enter the room. Everyone would come to attention and all sorting and work would come to a screeching halt. As a result, the loud arguing usually turned into whisper arguing.

Few people in the group believed we weren't working as a team. Constant blame was placed on some individuals who had a tendency to always get in trouble by the upperclassmen. As a result, we would try to make them the sorters, while the guys who had a better reputation would constantly leave the room in an effort to pass through the grips of the door-watchers. This would only work for about ten minutes before the upper class would demand to know why the same fifteen people were always delivering laundry.

After a few months, one of my good friends developed a plan. His name was Brice Hansen, and he was prior-enlisted in the Army. He believed that if we focused on the strengths and weaknesses of the group, the laundry could be delivered much faster. In order to implement his plan, he first reviewed the idea with all the plebes.

As all thirty of us were packed into the little room and ready to start that night, Brice said, "All right, guys. I've got this idea of how to get this done without any problems tonight."

Everyone, very skeptical of Brice's plan, listened as he continued.

"First, I think we need to send people out in teams of six or more in order to task-saturate the upper classes' ability to stop so many of us. This way, if one guy gets stopped, the rest of the group can continue delivering their packages. In fact, I think we should actually use one person as a guinea pig to draw attention away from the others. In order to keep the laundry in rank order, we'll purposely plug one member of each delivery team with an untucked shirt or something that will draw attention to him. Once the upper class singles him out, the rest of the deliverers can continue with their mission. This guy's job will be to keep the upper class busy while the rest of the plebes leave the room unnoticed. In an effort to not single out the same guinea pig each time, we'll change up who's responsible for keeping the upperclassmen busy."

As Brice finished communicating the idea, suddenly all the plebes were listening very closely. Everyone liked his idea and really thought it might work.

As the first group of six plebes lined up at the exit, ready to test the idea, we made sure the first guy had a messed-up belt. Scott, my roommate, was quick to volunteer for the duty of being the test dummy. In order to draw attention to Scott, we twisted his belt off to the right side before he exited the room. As the door flung open, Scott and the group of deliverers exited the room together. Inside the laundry room, we listened closely to see if anyone had been stopped. To our surprise, it only took three seconds from the time Scott walked out of the room before we heard an upperclassman.

"Montoya, stop!"

At this point we were all smiling with our ears to the door. We listened intently to the one-way conversation taking place in the hall.

"Did you not even check your uniform before you left the room?" the upperclassman questioned.

We all looked at each other with excitement, as we knew our plan had worked. As Scott was out in the hall getting drilled with questions, we quickly got the next team of six ready to exit the room. Luckily, we gave Scott the laundry bundle of the lowest-ranking upperclassmen in the company. This way, we could keep sending people out the door as Scott endured the wrath of the upper class.

Just as the new team was assembled, the other five who left the room with Scott finished their deliveries. As they walked in the door, the next six departed. This time we didn't even put a guinea pig in the group because Scott was doing such a good job of getting the upperclassmen's attention. They were really upset with his belt being off to the side. As the next group of six departed the room, not one of them was stopped, as all the focus was still on Scott. As we continued to execute the drill throughout the rest of the night, we knew our plan was working.

Duties that night were completed in less than forty minutes, which was a new record. This was the start of the creative thinking that took place, which drastically minimized the amount of time laundry duties took. After a while, we started holding competitions to see who could distract the upperclassmen the longest and produce the most number of laundry packages delivered.

* * *

The BLUF of this story is leaders always promote teamwork. At the heart of this principle is the idea that every member of the team has skills that can contribute to the success of the group.

The first few months at West Point proves to be a very hard transition for most people with respect to teamwork. Growing up in a society that preaches the importance of teamwork yet practices the mind-set of being an individual was a difficult concept to transition from. By nature, our minds are hardwired to have our own opinions and independent schemes for solving problems. Everyone always thinks they're a team player, but when push comes to shove, they are always taking care of themselves before anyone else. At the Academy, preaching teamwork and executing teamwork were one. Initially in the story, we were quick to blame each other for the failures of the group. Nothing would infuriate the upperclassmen more than poor teamwork. They understood its importance and necessity to leadership. If they ever heard arguing behind closed doors, they would immediately stop the transgression and punish the group for the actions of a few. To most, this might seem ridiculous, but to strong leaders, the punishment of the group was absolutely necessary. If there is one thing that West Point truly embodies, it's the absolute necessity of teamwork.

The failure of many leaders is their inability to cohesively utilize an individual's attributes for the success of the group. Some leaders are quick to only find reasons why a person can't contribute to the team. This way of thinking is counterproductive and needs to be reversed. When a leader takes charge of a group, he immediately needs to understand that every team member has positive attributes that can be extracted and applied to the team's success. Most of the time, extracting the positives from every member can be difficult. Some leaders are quick to give up on subordinates, and as a result, place greater responsibilities on the individuals who are more productive. This is a dangerous cycle that is counterproductive to the goals of the team. Two things happen when leaders make this decision. First, the team members that have no responsibilities become disgruntled and counterproductive as a result of their perceived inabilities to help the group. Second, the leader will see situations where these team members favor this decision because they now have fewer responsibilities. This scenario has a tendency to promote future behavior where reduced responsibility is sought in an effort to continually work less. In the story, Brice was the only person who believed every team member possessed strengths. Everyone in the group viewed getting stopped by an upperclassman as having a negative effect on the team. Behind closed doors, the individuals who had an affinity for causing this perceived negative action were ostracized within the group. It was the fundamental belief that Brice brought to the organization that changed the outcome of laundry duties. His leadership and ability to extract the strengths of all the members resulted in accomplishing our goal of shortening the amount of time in which laundry duty was conducted.

In the story, you could observe all the difficulties associated with team building. Despite our constant involvement with each other, the task of working together was very demanding. With that said, teamwork becomes even more difficult when individuals lack the ability to conduct business from the same location. With the development of new technology, teamwork is becoming more difficult for leaders to implement. Today, meetings can take place by video teleconferences, creating new challenges and endeavors. Leaders, in some instances, may be faced with situations where they have never even met members of their team. This is where a leader's ability to build a cohesive unit is more important than ever. Using numerous tools, leaders must implement creative thinking to ensure teamwork is never lost within their organization. Ironically, I'm going to look back to 1939 to demonstrate the importance of this potential shortfall that leaders might face. During this time, America was experiencing large-scale mobilization. Below is a speech given to the West Point graduating class of 1939 by Franklin D. Roosevelt. One can see even decades ago, this inspirational leader foresaw potential disconnect. He knew teamwork was going to become more difficult for future leaders as displacement occurred between organizations.

"Superintendent Benedict, Fellow Officers, Members of the Class of 1939... Leadership has meaning only as it brings about cooperation.

When men are working upon a great problem, but must work by themselves, or in small groups without close contact, there is danger that they may not pull in the same directions. Cooperation, therefore, means discipline, not meticulous through unthinking obedience to guardroom technique, nor blind mass cooperation of a Macedonian phalanx or the close-order attack. Discipline is the well-tempered working together of many minds and wills, each preserving independent judgment, but all prepared to sink individual differences and egotisms to attain an objective which is accepted and understood. When men are taken far apart by mechanics and specialization, teamwork is far more essential than when they are close together; for it must be teamwork of the mind as well as the body... There is no greater quality of discipline than the ability to recognize different techniques and different processes, and by persuasion and reason to bring these divergent forces into fruitful cooperation. You have seen the problem in its smaller aspects here at West Point. Let me commend to you in your Army careers a continuous study of problems outside as well as inside the military field, as the necessary preparation for the greatest success in your chosen work."

Franklin D. Roosevelt
President of the United States: 1933-1945
Graduation Address at West Point
June 12, 1939. (Peters, 1939)

3

SAMI

It was late on a Friday night at the United States Military Academy (USMA) when my roommate looked at me.

He said, "Preston, why the hell did we do this?"

It was a question that resonated through the halls of the school on an hourly basis, especially on the nights prior to a Saturday A.M. Inspection (SAMI). Luckily, Scott and I had managed to remain roommates after Beast Barracks, and this was yet another ordeal we would work through together. Along the way, we picked up another roommate, John David (JD) Galindo. JD was just like Scott and me with respect to his laid-back personality and affinity for avoiding trouble. About three times a semester, the senior leaders of the school would inspect all of the cadets' rooms on a Saturday morning. While most students at other colleges across the nation were partying and conducting themselves in ways we could only imagine, we were working frantically to clean our rooms. We had to pass the inspection's immaculate standards or else suffer the consequences. The next morning we would have at least fifty senior officers and cadets inspecting our room while we stood at attention behind our desks. The last thing we wanted was to draw attention to ourselves, because that always caused a snowball effect.

This was our first SAMI and we had heard horror stories about how hard it was. The punishment for not passing this inspection was to have our room in SAMI standards for a week. Based on the past six hours already spent cleaning our room that night, SAMI for a week was the last thing we wanted to endure during the academic year. It wasn't like our room was dirty; we were already getting inspected twice a day with AM Inspections (AMI) and PM Inspections (PMI). The SAMI was different from these other two; it was the big kahuna, the tidal wave of tidiness. Rumors were rampant with respect to the thoroughness of the examination. I heard all the inspectors would be wearing white gloves and would run their hands over every inch of our room. If any dust or dirt was left on their glove at the end of the inspection, it was game over. Even among the upperclassmen, the SAMI was dreaded.

At 11:30 p.m., Scott's team leader stopped by to give us a pre-inspection. Team leaders were from the sophomore class, and we commonly referred to them as Yuks instead of Yearlings. They were upperclassmen, but they weren't the yelling and screaming type. They had just finished their plebe year and were inclined to avoid such antics. Each Yearling was in charge of one plebe, and as a result, they were our true mentors and guides. They definitely weren't our friends, but they were some of the few upperclassmen we could go to with questions or advice. As Scott's team leader prepared to enter our room, he pushed open the door and looked at our name tapes hung on the outside.

After a brief pause, he looked at us in disgust and said, "So you three think you're ready to pass this inspection?"

We all three replied quickly, "Yes, Corporal."

He looked at us and just started shaking his head. "I thought you guys were down here cleaning," he said.

We all just smirked a little, because we thought he was joking with us. Sometimes the upperclassmen would try to make us laugh so they could yell at us when we didn't keep our composure. This wasn't the case with

Scott's team leader. At the same time we started to smirk, he put on a white glove and ran the tip of his finger across the top of our name tape that was hung on the outside of the door.

"If you don't clean a little faster, you might be dealing with SAMI for the next week," the team leader commented.

Our smirks turned to frowns in a matter of seconds. I couldn't believe it; he hadn't even walked through the door and already found dirt on the one-millimeter surface at the top of our name tape.

I could see the look on JD's face and I knew what he was thinking: "Who the hell would have looked there?"

The team leader quickly changed the tune of the conversation by saying, "Listen, I'm here to help you guys. I came down here to show you a couple of spots that you might have forgotten."

We all let out a sigh of relief as the team leader went throughout the room, showing us little horizontal surfaces that most wouldn't even think existed. Scott began taking notes on anything and everything his team leader said. We were so happy because getting help like this was something that normally didn't happen. It was like someone was showing us the answers to the test before we took it. Needless to say, our room, which we thought was spotless, yielded Scott's team leader two black gloves upon his departure. As soon as the team leader left the room, we all looked at each other in amazement.

Frustrated, JD said, "Mr. Clean, I mean Scott, could you pass me the bucket of water so I can wipe down the outside of this window?"

Even with the team leader's help, there was a problem with our room. This particular room had a monumental issue. It left us in such a quandary that we avoided the subject at all costs. As the night wore on, we became more involved with our cleaning and silence filled the room. It wasn't until two o'clock in the morning that we finally decided to call the cleaning operation quits and Scott broke the utter silence.

"Everything looks good, but how in the world can we cover up that smell?" JD and I just looked at Scott and shrugged our shoulders. We knew something needed to be done, but there really wasn't a solution.

"I have no clue. I think we're out of options," Scott said.

The last thing anyone wants to be is the smelly kid. We have all known people who just don't smell right. Even worse, we have all gone into a person's house that has a distinctive, terrible smell. At West Point, we call that funk.

Sometimes when I'd be standing in formation, I would hear an upperclassman say, "Where's that funk coming from?"

To the rest of the world, this translates into "Who's the smelly kid?" To sum things up, we had the funky room. We had a room that smelled worse than a ten-gallon drum of sour milk that had been roasting below our heater. We had been living in this horrible-smelling room for a month now, and despite our best efforts to blame one another, nothing could be done to diminish that awful odor. JD and I would constantly blame Scott, but he flipped out after a month and that was the end of the joke.

Deep down, JD and I knew it wasn't Scott, but we still liked to jag him about it. This smell wasn't even human. It was like something had died in our room, and there wasn't enough potpourri in the state of New York that could neutralize the power of this stink. Needless to say, it was embarrassing because we knew it wasn't a result of anything we were doing. Our laundry was done on time and we all had great hygiene, but that funk wouldn't leave the room. It worked on our behalf on a few occasions when an upperclassman would enter our room and ridicule us. He would be right in the middle of asking us knowledge or just wasting our time when the smell of the room would take over.

The upperclassman would be in mid-sentence when he would get a whiff of the room and say, "Oh, my God. What is that smell? I hate the smell of Plebes! Have fun soaking in the stink, you nasty plebes."

Most of the time, the upperclassmen would storm out of our room, cussing our names because of the terrible odor. It really didn't matter to us because it provided us with less time to endure endless questioning.

The smell might have worked well chasing unwanted visitors out of our room on random academic nights, but we all knew it was going to be a different story the next morning during the SAMI. The inspection was coming and we had no plan to fix the horrendous funk that permeated our room.

We slept well that night, despite using a small sleeping mat on the floor because we didn't want to loosen our tightly made beds. Sleeping in uncomfortable places became something we got used to. Oftentimes, plebes would sleep under their desks to avoid detection from the upper class. This would allow them a couple extra minutes to get some sleep, but it came with a huge price. This was a stunt that cadets had better be prepared to pay the consequences for if they were caught. We managed to get about three-and-a-half hours of sleep that night before the alarm went off at 5:30 a.m. The first thought that popped into my head that morning was SAMI.

Before the rigorous inspection was conducted, there were things that still needed to be taken care of. Since the inspection was after breakfast, we still needed to execute the morning routine of preparing for interrogation by the upper class. About thirty minutes before every morning formation, all the plebes would line up outside the rooms of their team leaders to conduct fourth class development time (FCDT). To prepare for FCDT, plebes would need to wake up at least an hour prior to their team leader's meeting time. This was a monotonous experience because every day I was required to memorize articles from the front page of "The New York Times," go over the number of days left before ten different events in the academic year, memorize the next four meals at the mess hall, and get a quick inspection of my uniform.

"The New York Times" portion wasn't a hard task because I was always interested in current events going on around the world. Normally, if a plebe had three articles memorized, he wouldn't need to worry about an upperclassman asking him for more information. The difficulty with corresponding with an upperclassman wasn't the knowledge, but rather using the approved format. For everything we said, there was a certain format that needed to be followed.

For example, if I said "Sir, in 'The New York Times' it was reported that President Bush met with the Foreign Ambassador to Pakistan to discuss relations in Afghanistan and the Middle East," I would be quickly stopped for using an inappropriate format. The proper format for discussing news with an upperclassman starts with, "Sir, *this morning* in 'The New York Times' it was reported that..." I was only asked about more than three articles a few times, and the punishment was well worth the compromise of an extra twenty minutes of sleep. The upperclassmen wanted to know dates, times, names, ranks, and even locations.

On the other hand, memorization of "The Days" was very meticulous. On a daily basis, one would need to memorize the number of days until the seniors received their class rings, the next home football game, the Army vs. Air Force football game, the Army vs. Navy football game, Christmas break, Yearling Winter Weekend, the

Five Hundredth Night Dance, the Army's birthday, the One Hundredth Night Dance, and Graduation. One might think it would be easy to just subtract one day from the previous number, but with so many dates and days that seemed to run together, it was very easy to forget which numbers I had memorized. Also, for the guys who were good at math, they couldn't remember the difference in days between events. For example, I know there are seventeen days between the Army vs. Navy game and Christmas break, so I just add the numbers as I recite the piece of knowledge. This didn't work, because I'd always get the jerk who would just want to know the days of one event, like the Winter Weekend Dance. This type of question would always put a foil in the number-counter's game. The only way to learn The Days was good old memorization every morning. The one bright spot regarding the memorization of The Days was that as the year progressed, there were fewer events to memorize.

Memorizing the next four meals was essential to a plebe's survival. This was the one topic that I was asked about more than anything else. Imagine a large senior football player getting out of class for the morning and wanting to know only one thing: what he would be eating for lunch. You better believe he would stop the first plebe he saw before every meal to know what was on the menu. The requirement for memorizing the meals was simple. You needed to know the main course, the drink, the side dish, and the dessert being served for the next four meals. The requirement was actually to know only the next three meals, but on occasion, you'd get the cruel upperclassman. He would ask a plebe what he was having for breakfast tomorrow - after just finishing breakfast. He wasn't breaking any rules. A plebe was required to know the next three meals, and technically, breakfast tomorrow, at 8:50 in the morning, was three meals away. Anyway, all this memorization and the meetings with the team leaders was an effort to prepare plebes for handling any questions they might have to endure throughout the day. All of this happened before breakfast formation and it was fast and furious.

After I had finished memorizing everything that morning, I slowly and exhaustively walked up to my team leader's door at 6:30 a.m. Lucky for me, she even needed to put some final touches on her room before the SAMI. As a result, I didn't have FCDT that morning and was able to go back to my room and clean further. At breakfast formation, the upperclassmen were quiet and didn't bother us very much. Most likely, they were tired from cleaning their own rooms all night. This was a rarity and we definitely enjoyed the change of pace, at least for as long as it lasted.

After breakfast, JD, Scott, and I hurried back to the barracks and conducted some last-minute cleaning before the SAMI. During the inspection, we were required to stand at attention behind our desks for the duration of the review.

Giving the room one last spray of air freshener before the start, Scott looked at us and said, "Maybe we should put our gas masks on and stand at attention behind our desks."

Needless to say, that helped ease the tension as we all stood worrying about the consequence of having the "funky room."

The preparation for SAMI was over. It was now time to get our legs ready to stand at attention for at least two hours as the entire chain of command inspected all of the rooms throughout the school. I was worried. I thought the room was extremely clean, but I knew the smell was going to wreak havoc on our reputation and potentially put us in SAMI for the entire week.

At the start of the inspection, we had some of the lower-ranking cadets come through the room. They were nicer than we had expected; this was an absolute surprise. We were expecting the usual routine in which an upperclassman would flip over our beds and blame it on our inability to make them tight enough. This was a standard technique so each inspector could then use the flipped bed as a tool for further destruction. To our dismay, none of these methods were happening.

We actually had one upperclassman leave the room and say, "This room looks OK and it's a pass. I have one thing, though. Montoya, stop making the room stink so bad."

Hearing this comment was like watching the floodwaters break through the Hoover Dam. There was absolutely nothing that could hold JD's composure as he kept his mouth shut with a colossal laugh building. As the insurmountable pressure grew, his nose gave way before his lips. As a result, a substantial amount of snot gushed out his nose and down his face. Scott, furious over the comment by the upperclassman, reveled in the punishment JD received for not keeping his composure. I just stood there enjoying the situation for what it was worth.

"Galindo, you think that's funny?" The upperclassman shouted. "Start The Days!"

As quickly as JD was unable to sustain the joke about Scott, he was starting the format for The Days.

"Sir, The Days, there are twenty-three-and-a-butt days until Army defeats Rutgers at Michie Stadium. There are forty-one-and-a-butt days until Army defeats Air Force..."

It was hard for Scott and me to keep a straight face as we watched JD passing the piece of knowledge with snot still running down the side of his face.

The upperclassman, bored with our antics, left the room as JD was still saying The Days. Many times an upperclassman would have us start a piece of knowledge and just leave as we were still talking.

After JD finished, he quickly wiped the side of his face and whispered underneath his breath, "That was worth it." This was a common phrase used by plebes after being punished for something stupid.

We couldn't talk because the door was open and there were upperclassmen constantly walking by, inspecting everything in sight. As silence permeated the room, we all started to ponder random thoughts. There was something different about this inspection. Even though we had never been through a SAMI before, it just didn't feel right. It was like the upperclassmen were being too nice. It almost seemed like something big was about to happen, but then again, it always seemed like something big was going to happen.

As I drifted off thinking about home and many other things, I heard an announcement come from the end of the hall.

"Company attention!"

We looked at each other quickly and realized what was happening. Anytime the company was called to attention it was because a high-ranking officer was entering the building. There was no way of telling who it was, but I expected a Lieutenant Colonel (LTC) at the least. A LTC is an officer who has either graduated from the Academy or ROTC and has served at least fifteen-plus years in the Army. These guys have a lot of authority and even make the upperclassmen tremble in their presence. I once saw a LTC give a senior cadet 100 hours of walking the area. As we listened closely to hear who might be coming, we could only hear a bunch of chatter. After about five minutes, I heard the sound of the most distinguishable voice at the entire school.

This wasn't an LTC; it was a Three-Star General. The Superintendent (SUPE) of West Point is a position given by Congress to a handpicked Three-Star General from the Army. The name of our SUPE was Lieutenant General

Daniel Christman. Talk about a whole new pucker factor. As soon as we heard his voice, Scott reached below his desk and pulled out the air freshener. Not even caring if any upperclassmen saw him out of the position of attention, he started spraying down the room like a world-class graffiti artist. By the sound of the SUPE's voice, he was at least five doors down the hall. How embarrassing. It's one thing to have upperclassmen, whom we don't even like, tell us our room stinks, but what was the SUPE going to think? There was no way this was going to be a good situation.

As we heard the SUPE get closer to our room, our hearts sank with the anticipation of what was upon us. He was only one door away and we knew the inevitable was going to occur. The SUPE was coming to our rotten, rancid-smelling room. Within minutes, the guessing game of his arrival was over.

"Gentlemen, how are we doing today?" the SUPE said as he entered our room.

"Great, Sir," we all quickly responded in unison.

As he walked around our room with his entourage of Colonels and Lieutenant Colonels, the SUPE looked at the three of us with a grin.

He said, "What do you guys call that smell?"

He hadn't even made it three steps inside the door and the terrible smell of the room had already assailed his nostrils. Stunned and worried, JD and I looked at each other.

Before we could respond, Scott blurted out, "Sir, we call it potpoushit. It's a touch of potpourri mixed with the smell of dead animal that's stuck in the rafters between the walls."

I couldn't believe my ears! Did he really just say that to a Three-Star General? You could see JD's head and eyes begin blinking and twitching in disbelief. This wasn't going to be SAMI for the week; it was going to be

SAMI for the rest of the year!

To our immense surprise, Scott's comment sparked laughter among the Army's proven leaders, and it actually lightened the mood of the entire room.

The one Colonel said to the SUPE, "Sir, I really think there is something dead in this room."

The SUPE, nodding his head in agreement, looked at the three of us with a smile and said, "Gentlemen, do you seriously think there is something dead in your room?"

Scott, our self-appointed spokesman, quickly responded. "Sir, we have been living in this room for the past month, our hygiene is great, our laundry is done on time, and yet that smell will not leave this room. When we first moved here, it already had the odor that you smell now. I am convinced that there is something wrong with the room that is beyond our control."

Scott had a way of expressing himself well, especially to senior officers. JD and I just stood there, scared and worried that we might say something to upset the General. After hearing Scott's comments, the General looked around the room as if he was pondering the task of defeating a foreign country in combat.

"Colonel," the General said, "What's the largest-sized animal that could get into the wall?"

"Probably a rat, Sir," the Colonel said.

The General continued, "A rat, huh? Well, by the smell of this room, there is no way a dead rat is in between the walls. My bet is a rat died behind that heater in the wall over there."

Pausing briefly to consider the correctness of his conclusion, the General then continued.

"I want that rat pulled out of that heater by Monday morning."

"Yes, Sir!" the Colonel barked back.

Without any hesitation, the General gave the room one last look and started to exit.

On his way through the door he said, "Have a good day, gentlemen. Your room looks great."

Chills ran down our spines. We could not believe the words that had come out of the SUPE's mouth. JD and I just looked at Scott, who wore an enormous grin, as we shook our heads in amazement at his earlier comments.

JD said to Scott, "Man, you should be a politician with that silver tongue."

Two days later, it was Monday morning and we were walking back from breakfast. As we entered our room, there stood two contractors with our massive heater pulled out of the wall and sitting on the floor.

"Hey, guys," the contractors said to us as we entered the room with puzzled looks on our faces.

"We are here to get the dead rat out of your heater," the one man commented.

"So you actually found a dead rat back there?" Scott asked.

"We sure did. It was enormous too! I don't know how you guys lived with that awful smell in here. We think it came in over the summer while the building was being renovated," he explained.

As I leaned behind the contractor and looked inside a white bucket that was sitting on the floor, I saw this ghastly unctuous rat. I couldn't believe the General had solved the problem within a couple of seconds, which had puzzled the entire chain of command for a month.

* * *

The BLUF of this story is twofold. First, leaders who take the time to pay attention to details save considerable amounts of time in the long run. Second, subordinate leaders who identify problems and solutions and address their concerns with their senior leadership often gain the respect of their superiors and see direct results from their correspondence.

Details, details, details. To most, details are something that perpetually annoy those who follow. To a follower, details are the things that slow down the progress of a mediocre project. Details are the afterthoughts; they are the extras that followers don't have time to execute. With that said, one must avoid the leader who gets bogged down in the details and doesn't understand the overall goal or mission. There's always balance to any argument, but with respect to the point I'm making, a strong leader understands the overall goal, yet considers all the finite details at the same time. In the story presented, the mission was to pass the SAMI. JD, Scott, and I had to stay focused on every detail of the room in order to prevent the pain of being under SAMI for a week. Some of our classmates didn't understand the concept of being detail oriented. As a result, they lost a lot of free time and evenings away from academics, cleaning their rooms for SAMI. The learning point relates to a much broader spectrum than the small instance demonstrated in this story. Detail-oriented leaders produce far greater profits/products than individuals who only focus on broad ideas. One's ability to focus on the details is obviously a function of time, but when extra time isn't spent on details, the results are drastically different. I think the guys who had to experience SAMI for a week got to bed at an early 11:30 p.m. The attention to details obviously made a difference to us that day.

For a person who has never been in the military, Scott's comments to the General might not appear to be a big deal. I'm here to tell you, this was definitely out of the ordinary. I'm sure many people have seen individuals in the workplace who are afraid to give their superiors negative information. They'll use ambiguous language like a Hollywood prenuptial agreement. Based on their input, superiors might believe business is going well when in actuality, the company is losing money each quarter. This is something that strong leaders need to avoid at all costs. Looking back at the story, Scott looked at the event as an opportunity opposed to an unlucky experience. He seized the moment and turned a terrible situation into one that fixed a serious problem. If the General would have asked JD or me what was causing the smell, we would have answered, "No excuse, Sir," and braced for the punishment. Leaders seize every opportunity with their superiors and address both problems and successes. Below is a very important speech that the Secretary of Defense gave to the Corps of Cadets on 21 April 2008 pertaining to the same subject I'm highlighting. This is a terrific story.

"One thing will remain the same. We will still need men and women in uniform to call things as they see them and tell their subordinates and superiors alike what they need to hear, not what they want to hear.

Here, too, George Marshall in particular is a worthy role model. In late 1917, during World War I, the U.S. military staff in France was conducting a combat exercise for the American Expeditionary Force commander. General Pershing was in a foul mood. He dismissed critiques from one subordinate officer after another. But then – Captain Marshall took the arm of the four-star general, turned him around, and told him how the problems they were having resulted from not receiving a necessary manual from the American headquarters – Pershing's headquarters. The commander said, 'You know we have our troubles.' Marshall replied, 'Yes, I know you do General... But ours are immediate and every day and have to be solved before night.' After the meeting, Marshall was approached by other officers offering condolences for the fact that he was almost sure to be fired and sent off to the front line. Instead, Marshall became a valued advisor to Pershing, and Pershing a valued mentor to Marshall. Twenty years later, then-General Marshall was sitting in the White House with President Roosevelt and all of his top advisors and Cabinet secretaries. War in Europe was looming, but still a distant possibility for an isolated America. In that meeting, Roosevelt proposed that the U.S. Army – which at that time ranked in size somewhere between that of Switzerland and Portugal – should be of lowest priority for funding and industry. FDR's advisors nodded. Building an Army could wait.

Then FDR, looking for the military's imprimatur to his decision, said: 'Don't you think so George?' Marshall, who did not like being called by his first name, said: 'I am sorry, Mr. President, but I don't agree with that at all.' The room went silent. The Treasury Secretary told Marshall afterwards: 'Well, it's been nice knowing you.' It was not too much later that Marshall became the Army Chief of Staff."

Secretary of Defense Robert Gates
The West Point Evening Lecture,
delivered at West Point
April 21, 2008. (Gates, 2008)

Preparing for SAMI with Scott Montoya and J.D. Galindo

4

The Aussie's Posse

Everyone knows that guy — the guy in the crowd of people who just stands out. I'm not talking about the person who stands out for inferior reasons, but instead, the person who stands out because everyone wants to be around him. I was at West Point for about one month when I came across that guy. His name was Mitch Rosnick and he was different to say the least. Not in a bad way, but in a fascinating way. People clung to this guy like he was a prophet. During Beast Barracks, which was a time when no one knew anyone's personality, this Rosnick guy was a standout. It was like everyone was in formation and this one guy could march to the beat of his own drum. He was about 5'11" with brown hair, brown eyes, and a moderate build. His appearance was similar to any other cadet attending the Academy, yet he possessed this bubble that attracted anyone around him to join his team.

My first memory of New Cadet Rosnick was when our company had a competition to see who could disassemble and reassemble an M16 rifle the fastest. Drills and competitions were always a great break from the monotony of our typical training during Beast. It was a brief amount of time where we could show our personalities and competitive spirit. As the tournament began, each internal squad held its own timed rivalry. Then the squads would compete against each other. After only a couple minutes, the contest had worked through the squads like the brackets of March Madness; winners and losers were quickly emerging throughout and hundreds of new cadets were competing. After an aggressive battle to the final bout, there were only five cadets vying for the championship, and Rosnick was one of them.

As the upperclassmen gathered all the new cadets around the final five contenders, the time keeper quickly silenced the crowd.

He shouted, "On your marks, get set, go!"

When I watched Rosnick disassemble and reassemble his weapon, I couldn't help but notice the crowd of cadets that was standing behind him. He had loyal comrades who were going well out of their way to promote his winning. Relative to the other new cadets competing for the title of being the fastest weapon assembler that summer, no one had nearly gathered the support and veneration that Rosnick had acquired. It was like Rosnick was their chosen leader, their deity; his classmates would have followed him anywhere. As the final bolts were fastened into place, there was one man standing: Rosnick. I was obviously amazed at his lightening speed, but I was more amazed at the crowd of people that picked this guy off his feet and into the air like a piece of popcorn being carried by 10,000 ants. The upperclassmen quickly put an end to the craziness, but the chaos that this guy created lived in my mind forever. I remember thinking, *how could a guy cultivate a clique in such a short amount of time under the conditions we had been living under?* They didn't hoist him into the air because he had won; they lifted him higher because his supporters revered him. By the end of the Beast Barracks summer training, Rosnick was selected by the upperclassmen as the best new cadet out of all my classmates. This guy was quickly making a name for himself.

For the rest of my plebe year I didn't really see Rosnick except for casually passing him on my way to class. All alone, I would pass him like every other cadet. He, on the other hand, would always have an entourage of at least five people walking behind his lead. I would often smile and think to myself, *what is that guy selling?* For me, it was really funny to see, because I didn't personally know him, and yet it seemed as if people treated him like a celebrity. Out of my 1,000 classmates, I never talked to the guy, yet I knew his name as well as I knew my best friends' names.

A year later, it was my second summer of military training at Camp Buckner. At this point I still didn't know Rosnick, but when he won the Sean Knott Ranger Buddy Award, I knew there was something very special about this guy. This was the top award given to the number one cadet during our second summer of training. After Camp Buckner was completed that summer, I was reassigned to a new company for the academic year. Essentially, all the students are assembled into thirty-two companies. A good way to understand the company structure is to envision each company as a fraternity. These were the people we lived and worked with on a daily basis. We knew some cadets outside our company, but the cadets inside our company were the ones we knew extremely well. In an effort to give plebes a new start as upperclassmen, the school scrambled all freshmen from their original plebe year companies. In my new company, I was assigned to live with a guy named Jack Johannes. At first glimpse, Jack is a tall, 6'4" monster who had a very intimidating personality. He was definitely more military-like than my old roommate, Scott. It was going to be interesting to see how things worked out with Jack. In addition to my new roommate, I also happened to get scrambled to the same company as this renowned Rosnick character. Immediately, I was interested in knowing what all the fuss was about. What made this guy tick?

During the first week back in the barracks, now as an upperclassman, I couldn't help but enjoy the exhilarating and foreign experience. Instead of avoiding everyone who walked the halls, I now found myself like all the other upperclassmen, enjoying the camaraderie of company living. It didn't take more than a couple days before I decided to walk over to Rosnick's room to introduce myself. As I got close to his room and was about to open the door, I was startled to see it flung open. To my surprise, I saw an up-armored Rosnick emerge from his room with an M4 Carbine Rife. The rifle had a laser-designated scope, a flashlight mounted to the hand guards, and an extendable butt stock. He was dressed in all black and had a pistol mounted to the side of his leg. Somewhat frightened and astonished at the same time,

Rosnick whispered to me, "Hey, mate. I need you to do me a solid and take this little pee shooter and shoot the first bloody bloke walking down the hall. As for me, I'm popping smoke and flanking his movement."

Looking at this Rosnick guy like *you've got to be out of your mind*, I unthinkingly raised my hand and took the pistol that he had pulled out of his hip carrier. I thought to myself, *what kind of English is this guy speaking?* He sounded like the announcer from the TV show "Lifestyles of the Rich and Famous." The whole situation was just really bizarre. Rosnick could obviously tell by the look on my face that I thought the weapon was real. Quickly and quietly, he assured me that it was a BB gun that only looked real and wouldn't pierce the skin. In disbelief, I popped the clip out of the pistol and realized he was telling the truth. Having been at the school for one year, I had a fair amount of time handling different weapons. So when I felt this BB pistol, the weight and aesthetics were comparable to any real weapon I had handled in the past. This thing was awesome! I could only imagine what his fully automatic BB M4 rifle was capable of doing. Within seconds, I was part of Rosnick's team, ready for what seemed to be a S.W.A.T. attack against some of his friends.

As I got down on one knee to discuss the plan with Rosnick, I saw his roommate emerge from the room with a weapon that looked just like an MP5 fully automatic rifle. I couldn't believe my eyes. These weapons looked so real. There were definitely no red caps on the ends of these toy guns. Rosnick's roommate passed him another clip for his M4. I just stayed kneeling on the ground, thinking about how hilarious the whole situation was. As we all huddled up, Rosnick quickly took over as the team leader. He calmly and collectively started giving orders.

"New guy, I want you to remain right here in this hallway because it's tucked away from the main avenue of approach. When they make the turn to come into my room, I want you to initiate fires on the enemy. They don't know you, so they won't suspect the attack. As for us, we'll be in the room right down the hall. As soon as we hear you initiate the attack, we'll use the power of our fully automatic weapons to waste them from the flank. Does anyone have any questions?"

I hesitated a little bit and looked at Rosnick and said, "Um...yeah. Do these things hurt?"

They just laughed and ignored my question. Thinking that I was joking, Rosnick continued.

"All right. I got word from my intel (intelligence) source that they'll be here in about five minutes, so let's get in position."

As soon as Rosnick was done talking, he and his roommate executed their movement to the room right down the hall. After they left me alone, I couldn't help but reminisce on how I found myself in this situation within seconds of trying to introduce myself. Here I was, kneeling in the corner of this little hallway, holding an electric pistol that shoots plastic BB's at a speed that will surely leave welts all over the body. I didn't know who or what was coming my way. All I knew was Rosnick and his roommate were on my side. All I could hope for was not getting hit. The spot I was hiding in was a very good place to be, but I felt all alone in the dark, narrow hallway.

After only a couple minutes, I heard some whispering coming from around the corner. I slowly moved my pistol to the ready position as I continued to hear the enemy prepare to make the turn around the corner of the hall. I watched intently as I saw the barrel of someone's weapon breach the corner of the wall. As the person's body quickly emerged from the corner, I began to fire my pistol directly into his chest. Immediately, he began to spray BB's from his automatic weapon in self-defense. Lucky for me, he wasn't looking where his weapon was aimed and the BB's all missed. Within seconds of hearing the fired shots in the hall, Rosnick and his roommate kicked open the door directly behind the attackers' position and began to spray the enemy with hundreds of BB's. After being pelted with numerous small rounds, the attackers quickly retreated. They looked like a bunch of wounded dogs with their tails between their legs as they ran away.

After the successful mission, Rosnick and his roommate came over with big smiles on their faces, laughing uncontrollably.

His roommate said, "Hey, man. That was awesome. You did a great job. Thanks for helping us out. My name is Alex, how about you?"

Laughing with them I said, "Thanks, that was hilarious. My name is Preston." Then Rosnick replied, "Hey, mate. My name is Mitch. Why don't you come into our room so we can chat some more?"

Exhilarated from the first ten minutes of knowing Mitch and Alex, I walked into their room and bombarded them with questions.

The first and obvious question I had for them was,

"Who the hell were those guys?"

They just laughed and Mitch said, "Oh, those were some of my friends from my old company. We've been having these little attacks all week. The only problem for them is I have some friends in their company and they keep tipping me off. They tell me every time they are about to attack."

I started laughing and quickly fired off another question, "OK, what is up with your accent? Are you from Australia or something?"

"I sure am," Mitch said. With a look of confusion on my face, I questioned further.

"OK, then how are you here at West Point?"

Mitch could tell I was confused, so he explained the whole story of how he ended up at the Academy.

Evidently, Mitch's mother is Australian and his father is American, which made him a dual citizen. After finishing high school and growing up in Australia, one of his friends was living in the United States and had joined the U.S. Army. His friend had called Mitch, telling him how he absolutely loved being in the Army. After his friend bragged about all the weapons and tanks he was getting to shoot and drive, Mitch was drawn to undergo similar experiences for himself. After enlisting in the Army, Mitch was assigned to South Korea where he became a Sergeant and Tank Commander by the age of 20. Since he showed so much potential, his chain of command encouraged him to apply to West Point. After a long and arduous application process, Mitch found himself far from his original desire to be driving tanks and shooting guns and instead found himself in low-quarter shoes and a black necktie, going to one of the strictest colleges in America. As I sat listening to my two new friends, I couldn't help but feel welcomed into this Aussie's posse. In a short amount of time, I felt like I had known Mitch and Alex my entire life.

As the year progressed, Mitch and I became really good friends. He was the guy a person could always turn to when things weren't going well. It was at this point that it became very clear why he attracted friends like mosquitoes flying around a light pole. Not only was his personality bigger than life, but he was one of the most honest and trustworthy guys I knew.

As Yearlings, we really didn't have many privileges. We were upperclassmen, but we still couldn't leave the post on weekdays. In fact, our rights on the weekends were almost as minimal as the weekdays. For some guys, these rules were very difficult to obey; Mitch happened to be one of those guys. My personal opinion of why it was so hard for Mitch was because he was older than most of our classmates. I was only 20 years old, whereas Mitch was 25 and much more mature. He had already been deployed overseas and led Soldiers. He was of drinking age and experienced many things that I didn't even know existed. Regardless of the reasons, Mitch felt like a caged animal locked inside the institution's doors. For Mitch, if rules or standards didn't make any sense, he had no problems breaking them.

Mitch told me that it started off simple and more like an experiment than anything else. Early in the first semester of our Yearling year, Mitch decided to see if he could leave the post without getting caught. He didn't plan on making a habit of leaving; he just wanted to see if it was possible. He was a very adventurous guy and liked to test the limitations of restrictions. So after drumming up enough courage, Mitch just walked off the post. In order to protect his insubordination, he wore his physical training uniform so no one could recognize his rank. After passing the gate guard with pure confidence, the rest of the journey was easy. He walked around the small town of Highland Falls like a pet that was accidentally let out of the fence that surrounds the yard. He didn't go far, yet he still showed consideration for the potential trouble if caught. His first little adventure of leaving post was spent just going to grab something to eat, but his tryst was destined to evolve into something of more epic proportions.

After his first little adventure, Mitch couldn't believe how easy it was to just blend in. He found that people off the base were a lot less interested in his behavior than he thought. Although everyone off the post didn't care about his actions, the leaders within the institution would surely feel different if they knew about his insubordination. Essentially, once a cadet becomes a junior, or Cow, he is rewarded by the privilege of being able to leave the post during the evening of any weekday or weekend. As cadets, we called this new benefit the "off-post privilege pass," or OPP for short. This was a huge deal and something that all the cadets anticipated for two years. For Mitch, he felt this rule was completely absurd and it didn't pass the commonsense test. As a result, he developed his own rule and commonly referred to his new benefit as BPP; that is, the "blow-post privilege pass."

As I mentioned earlier, living in a company was like living with a family. In order to conduct parties and provide food at our company store, money needed to be raised. One of the more unique ideas that our company developed in order to raise money was to conduct an auction. It was very funny to see some of the items that people provided for the fund-raiser. The seniors, or Firsties, actually auctioned their rank for a day. This undoubtedly excited all the plebes because it allowed them to boss all the upperclassmen around for a day. Some plebes were willing to pay more than $100 to be treated like an upperclassman for just one day. Despite what many might think, the upperclassmen honored the privilege if a plebe was willing to contribute so much money to the company's funds. One of the most surprising items that was auctioned was when our tactical officer decided to sell a get out of jail free card. Essentially, the card would dismiss any cadet from a company- level disciplinary board. This quickly became a very valuable item to numerous cadets in our company who had recently gotten themselves into trouble. As the auction began, everyone in the company immediately recognized the individuals vying for the item. With that said, everyone was surprised to see Mitch raising the ante. After only a few seconds, they knew what he was doing. He was clearly trying to acquire the get out of jail free card in order to flip a profit to an upperclassman. He was always thinking in creative ways.

As the semester progressed, Mitch continued to become more daring. He started off simple, but slowly moved on to more mischievous actions. In an effort to see how far he could take the charade, Mitch decided to start wearing civilian clothes when leaving the post. This was obviously a more daring move, considering the punishment would be double for breaking two rules. All these rules really didn't scare Mitch very much. Some might argue this was the reason he wasn't getting caught. His laid-back personality and no-fear approach seemed to be fooling everybody. The most amazing aspect of Mitch's ability to fool the upperclassmen was the fact that he wore civilian clothes right out of his room. This might not sound unusual to most, but considering our class wasn't even allowed to keep civilian clothes in our room, it should have set off alarm bells for everyone to hear. I remember walking out of the bathroom and seeing Mitch dressed like an upperclassman getting ready to take his BPP. I could not understand how a person could get away with the things he was doing. As luck had it, Mitch successfully continued to dupe the system, even while wearing civilian clothes. His actions were so blatant that it almost seemed like he was trying to get caught.

Before long, it became very common for Mitch to

leave the post and enjoy his night out. In fact, he began renting cars on the weekends in order to travel to some of his favorite spots along the Hudson River. As a native of Australia, he obviously loved barbecue, so when he found a restaurant in Newburgh called Barnstormers BBQ, he instantly fell in love. This was a place where he could wash his worries away. The only problem for Mitch was the barbecue was a forty-five-minute drive from the Academy. The ante of his quest now held a higher price. The only way Mitch was able to continue frequenting his favorite restaurant was to own his own car. After some covert research, he discovered a 1986 Chevy Camaro that was owned by a Department of Defense (DOD) civilian. This is the point where Mitch began to lose focus on his original intent. Instead of testing the system, he was clearly breaking the rules. Instead of taking casual strolls in the nearby town, he was now intending to drive his newly acquired car to cities well outside the local area. As if leaving post without a pass wasn't bad enough, having his own car as a third-class cadet was an obvious violation of even more rules. If caught, there was going to be a severe price to pay. Punishment for breaking this many rules was surely going to give Mitch at least 100 hours of marching in the area. Marching off that many hours would take every weekend for an entire semester. He clearly knew the stakes were very high.

Mitch's luck was bound to end soon, but based on his past experience, fear gradually slipped away from reality. It was a Tuesday night and Mitch had just finished his classes for the day. He decided to get three of his closest friends and leave post in his new Camaro. The night was going great. Having been a loyal customer at his favorite restaurant allowed him to be on great terms with one of the more attractive waitresses. So when he walked in and got seated immediately among a busy crowd of customers, his friends were immediately impressed. Unfortunately for Mitch, so was his Beast Barracks platoon sergeant who was eating just three tables away. The upper-class cadet was now a senior and clearly knew Mitch lacked the privileges to be off post and eating in a town thirty miles away. As Mitch took his seat, he gave a slow nod to the upper-class cadet like a cowboy from the Wild West. There was no duel that night, but the constant and profound stares were enough to cut the tension with a knife. At this point, Mitch decided he shouldn't let the situation potentially ruin his last night out. When the waitress came back to take their orders, Mitch decided there was only one rule left to break. So he ordered himself a nice tall glass of beer to go with his side order of fear and regret.

After returning to the base that night, it only took a couple of minutes to check his e-mail and identify a letter from the upperclassman he saw at the restaurant. Hoping for the best, Mitch knew he needed to expect the worst. After opening the document he read a brief message.

Cadet Rosnick,
You are not an upperclassman. You do not have the privileges of an upper-class cadet. I will be reporting your behavior to your chain of command for breaking the rules.

It was short, it was simple, and it was definitely to the point. It only took about twenty minutes after reading the e-mail for a member of Mitch's chain of command to come knocking at the door. The company's first sergeant, John Morris, didn't waste any time in his attempt to tactically question Mitch about his night out.

"Word has it you blew post tonight, Rosnick," Morris said. "Why don't you tell me all the details?"

Without hesitation, Mitch responded, "Yeap, you got that right. I was out and having a great time tonight. You should have been there. We got ourselves some drinks and found ourselves some ladies... You know, John, you look so upset, maybe you should have come with us."

Furious and frustrated with Mitch's eloquent honesty, First Sergeant Morris was in no mood to be putting up with such antics.

"You said 'we.' What did you mean by that?" Morris aggressively replied.

"Well, if you think I'm going to tell you that, you must be out of your bloody mind," Mitch said calmly.

Although Mitch had broken numerous rules, there was one thing that he understood very well: His honor could not be used against him. He had been caught redhanded, and as a result, was more than willing to take the punishment for the crime. One thing he was not willing to do was snitch on his best friends.

Morris, realizing he wasn't getting anywhere with his interrogation, decided to upgrade the level of visibility for Mitch's actions.

The next day was extremely brutal for Mitch. First Sergeant Morris had followed through with his threat and had reported Mitch's insubordination through the entire chain of command. Before talking to Morris, it was just cadets who were involved, but after refusing to turn in his friends, the upperclassmen got regular Army officers involved in the quandary. If he would have only cooperated with John Morris, his punishment would have stayed at the company level. Instead, he was now going to be punished at the regimental level, and that meant 100 hours or more.

Although Mitch had been breaking numerous rules, his charismatic character was something that many held on high. The members of the numerous clubs Mitch was actively involved in provided him with an added benefit. As a member of the combat weapons team and the pistol club, he had friends who were high-ranking cadets in the chain of command. In fact, a few friends were first-class cadets on the regimental staff. As most might suspect, they weren't nearly as upset as First Sergeant Morris. With a little persuasion and Australian charm, Mitch was able to convince his upper-class friends to downgrade his punishment to only a company-level board. In the four years I attended the Academy, I never saw someone with so many connections. Mitch truly was "that guy."

As many might suspect, when Mitch's punishment returned to the company level, First Sergeant Morris and the rest of the chain of command were anxious to issue his punishment. They looked at Mitch like a convict who was always able to evade prosecution. This time they were the judge and they were ready to be relentless. It was a couple days later when the company decided to hold the board to determine Mitch's fate. The company tactical officer, the cadet company commander, and the cadet company first sergeant all salivated prior to the start of the board. As Mitch entered the room, they instructed him to remain at the position of attention while they began their verbal lashings. At the start, they reviewed all of the rules that Mitch had broken. As they progressed, the assault became more aggressive. They assured him he would receive the maximum number of hours walking the area, along with numerous "special" projects that needed to be completed in the company area. The board lasted a half hour, and during that entire time, Mitch never spoke a word. As the prosecutors made their final remarks, the tactical officer asked Mitch if he had anything to say.

At this point, Mitch slowly reached in his back pocket and pulled out his wallet. Inside, he slowly unfolded a little card that read, "One get out of jail free card for any company-level board."

As he gently placed the card on the officers' table, Mitch said, "If there is one thing I won't be having, it's all that stuff you guys have been talking about for the last thirty minutes."

Absolute silence filled the room as the prosecutors' minds raced like wild horses.

At this point, Mitch officially became a company legend. Everyone in the room knew they had been duped. He had (literally) played his card so eloquently that everyone was flabbergasted.

The commander was so furious he screamed, "Get out of my office, now! We will talk about this later."

As Mitch left the commander's office, he knew he had won. They both knew Mitch couldn't be punished. Hell, the card was signed by the same commander who was giving him the tongue lashing. Although he was promised that they would talk about the incident later, that never happened. Mitch had officially blown post and thumbed his nose at all the rules and never paid any price. More importantly, he did this without jeopardizing his integrity or friends.

* * *

The BLUF of this story is that leaders of character are the most valuable assets of any organization.

After reading this story, many might anticipate that my summary of Mitch's integrity will be reviewed negatively. In fact, I propose the contrary in an effort to highlight the differences between character and poor decision-making. First and foremost, Mitch's actions to break the rules were a poor choice, and he should have endured the punishment that the chain of command decided was appropriate. With that said, there is a very distinct and defined difference between Mitch's core decision to break the rules and his unwavering integrity to maintain accountability of the truth. His ability to always place his honor first, regardless of the potential punishment, is the keystone of this chapter. A great quote that paints the canvas of this representation comes from the billionaire investor Warren Buffett. He says, "Your character is like fine china. It takes a lifetime to acquire, but five seconds to destroy." I think everyone can agree that Mitch could have destroyed his character in five seconds if he had tried to lie about his poor decisions.

Why do people lie? This is something that everyone must understand in order to conquer the poisoning habit. The answer to the first question is quite simple: People destroy their character because they do not want to endure the punishment that is associated with their poor decisions/actions. In short, they seek to gain an unfair advantage. Children lie to their parents about taking a cookie because they do not want to stand in the corner for twenty minutes. Teenagers lie to their school teacher about missing class because they do not want to get detention. Adults lie to their boss about using company funds because they do not want to get fired. Regardless of the age or circumstances, people lie because they are unwilling to pay the price for their poor decisions. This is what made Mitch different from most people. This is why the Aussie's posse would follow him anywhere. If there's one thing Mitch possessed, it was integrity.

When I started creating this chapter, I contacted Mitch about my interest in writing about this particular story. Initially, when I asked for his permission, he was a little nervous. Looking back on the whole story, Mitch was not very proud of his decision to break the rules. With that said, I felt that it was a great story because it provided a discernable difference between poor decision-making and integrity. Additionally, I assured Mitch that most people reading the book probably wouldn't discredit his "poor decision" as harshly as the West Point tactical officers — especially considering he was 25 years old and just wanted to have his own car and eat some barbecue.

In the story, Mitch's choice to take a harder right

instead of the easier wrong is the hallmark of a strong leader. Punishment did not scare him. In fact, it almost seemed like Mitch sponsored castigation. When First Sergeant Morris questioned Mitch, he never hesitated when telling the truth. This was an interesting difference in behavior that I had not seen before attending the Academy. Cadets always seem so willing to step up and take punishment for even the smallest mistakes. In my humble opinion, this is the single greatest gift a cadet acquires from attending West Point.

The first week of attending the Academy, I was required to memorize the mission statement of the school. It read:

"The mission of the United States Military Academy is to educate, train, and inspire leaders of character for the Army and Nation."

At the time, the statement didn't mean nearly as much as it does now. The one word that really jumps out of the entire statement is the word "character." Speaking on behalf of all graduates, this is the word that truly is our rallying point.

Mitch Rosnick and Alex Garcia (Roomates)
Reunited in the mountains of Afghanistan - trading
in their B.B. guns for the real deal

Mitchell Rosnick

Since graduation, Captain Mitchell Rosnick has deployed to Iraq and Afghanistan as an OH-58 scout helicopter Platoon Leader and Commander. Some of his higher awards and decorations include: Bronze Star Medal, Air Medal, Joint Service Commendation Medal, Army Commendation Medal, Army Achievement Medal, Afghanistan Campaign Medal with combat star, Iraq Campaign Medal with combat star, Army Campaign Medal, Global War on Terror Medal, the National Defense Service Medal, and the Combat Action Badge.

Mitch Rosnick

5

Airborne

The wind was just right. There was a slight breeze from the north and the sun had just set. Although the sun was down, there was still enough light to videotape the daring event. The lack of illumination would work perfectly to hide the identity of the individuals involved, yet allow enough light for viewers to see the bold feat. As a masked cadet emerged at the top of the infamous clock tower, the cadet videotaping the event began recording. The enterprising cadet stood between the ramparts and was ready to help execute one of the most life-threatening airborne jumps in the history of the Academy. Instead of executing the jump himself, he forcefully pushed the daredevil forward. Staring down the steep five-story wall of Pershing barracks was enough to scare anyone for such a death-defying feat. More masked cadets waited at the bottom of the building, ready to provide support in the event of a catastrophe. As the cadets on the ground gave their thumbs up to execute the mission, the masked cadet on top of the clock tower gently threw the test dummy off the building. As she started falling toward the ground, the parachute opened and the rapid descent quickly decelerated. As the masked cadets at the base of the building prepared for the creature's landing, one individual caught the amiable hamster that completed its first airborne jump. Although few students were privy to the actual event, all cadets undoubtedly saw the video that was disseminated through e-mail like smuggled drugs.

The Airborne Hamster incident rapidly circulated through the Corps of Cadets. The tiny animal had so much stardom that everyone at the Academy talked about the enigma behind the whole incident. The episode created such a buzz that even professors knew about the occurrence. For most cadets, the most puzzling piece of the conundrum was where the masked cadets hid their hamster. With inspections occurring at least two times a day, the hamster was obviously hidden in an ingenious location in order to keep her away from inspecting officers. Additionally, everyone really wanted to find out who the masked cadets were. If the leader of the group were ever caught, it would surely result in numerous hours walking the area. I thought the incident was really funny and daring on the part of the individuals involved, but I had much more important things to worry about that week.

It was the second semester of my Yearling year and my academic classes were really starting to heat up. I was taking 22.5 credits in one semester and some of the classes were absolutely overwhelming. It was hard talking to friends at other universities who were full-time students and taking 12 credits. Combining the numerous classes with the rigorous physical and military requirements drastically increased the difficulty of the whole college experience. It was hard to relate to friends at other universities who complained because they had a class on Tuesday and Wednesday. West Point was more like high school with respect to the academic day being divided into periods. Ironically, there were no bells between classes, but every class would start and end exactly on the second. Every clock in the entire school was GPS timed, so there was never a good excuse for being late. If you were late, you walked hours. It was that simple. For this particular semester, I was taking seven classes, which demanded every ounce of attention in order to get a passing grade. I studied Portuguese, Engineering Mathematics, Perspectives on Officership, Physical Fitness and Health, Physics, Philosophy, and American Politics.

Across the ranks, grades were very important to all the cadets, and I was no different than the norm. As if the courses weren't difficult enough, the entire school used an amended grading scale in which 94%-100% was the category for an "A," 84%-93% was a "B," etc. Needless to say, there were many times I had a 93% in a class and received a "B+" for my final grade. This was very frustrating, coming from a public education system that was tailored toward the typical 10% scale. As I sat in my Portuguese class that afternoon, I looked around the room and had to laugh at what I saw. Of the fifteen cadets taking the course, six of them were out of their seats and standing in the back of the room. One was even sleeping while standing. This was a very common occurrence at the Academy. Instructors never minded the flock of cadets standing in the back of the room. They knew if we weren't allowed to stand, we would fall asleep at our desks. The subject could be exhilarating, but when a cadet is trying to stay awake after getting four hours of sleep a night, it becomes a very cumbersome task for students. As I looked at my classmates struggling to stay conscience, I heard the instructor make an announcement that we were going to have a test during the next lesson. Everyone's dazed stares quickly turned to frustrated grins as we heard the terrible news. My ears started turning red. I knew I was preparing for a catastrophic day. Based on the new requirement, I needed to study for four tests all on the same day. The only class I didn't have a test in was Engineering Math. This was a good thing, as this was the most difficult class and required the most preparation. Most cadets would estimate that for each hour of class, there's approximately two hours of homework. So fitting eight hours of homework into a night of studying was going to be a challenging task. Obviously, there wasn't enough time to study for all four requirements. As a result, I needed to prioritize which classes I could afford to get lower scores in. These classes would be the ones I would give the least amount of attention. I was performing well in my Physics and Philosophy class, so I could afford getting lower grades on those tests. It was the Portuguese and American Politics classes that I was worried about.

After classes finished that day, I hurried back to my room because I needed to prepare for drill practice. We typically had fifteen to twenty minutes to drop our bags at the room and get dressed in the proper uniform for drill. Drill is something that most people envision when they think about West Point. Pictures of the Academy always depict thousands of cadets marching on a big open field with rifles and parade hats. In order to teach this disciplined duty, we would typically practice drill for four to five hours a week. No one ever looked forward to drill. For anyone who has seen the Army-Navy football game, this is what I am referring to. Undoubtedly, cadets hate drill. This is the one thing they will try to avoid more than anything else. The only problem with avoiding drill is that it's almost impossible. The leaders know cadets try and avoid the mundane and disciplined duty, so there are rosters and strict attendance before every practice. As I scurried along to drill that afternoon, I could tell it was going to be the same monotonous marching patterns on the parade field. During the two-hour detail, all I could think about was the four tests I needed to study for that night. The last thing I wanted to do was march the countless circles around the parade field because I knew I'd be studying until at least 3 a.m. It was things like drill that made the Academy a difficult place to endure. In this particular situation, it was hard keeping a positive mindset. I wasn't going to get any sleep because I "wasted" all my time on the parade field. This is an idea that's very hard to put into text, but the constant battle of reality and perception, with respect to using one's time wisely, was a struggle for all cadets throughout the entire four years.

After dinner, I got back to my room at approximately 7:30 p.m. and immediately began studying. I started memorizing all the Portuguese vocabulary that I neglected over the last couple days because of numerous other academic requirements. Managing scholastics was like walking a tight rope while juggling eight bowling pins. For me, Portuguese was one of the eight bowling pins, but it was the hardest to catch. I mostly attributed my difficulties to the fact that I'm not a verbal-minded person. Since the time I was young, I always struggled with language-related studies. In high school, I was fortunate to take three years of Spanish, giving me a foundation for studying a foreign language. I would get "A's" and "B's" in high school Spanish, but when I started taking foreign languages in college, it was much more demanding. One might wonder why I was taking Portuguese instead of Spanish, especially considering I already had three years of experience. For this simple fact, I can only blame myself. During the first month at the Academy, we actually picked which foreign language we wanted to study. Needless to say, I was very motivated and somewhat arrogant in my ability to learn. As a result, I ended up picking Portuguese instead of Spanish. I thought it was an interesting language and I wanted to learn something new. The only problem was I didn't realize it was so similar to Spanish. In fact, it was too similar. One might think this would be a good thing, but for me it wasn't. By the end of my year of learning Portuguese, I think I spoke Spanuguese. I would constantly mix up the words and sentence structure between Spanish and Portuguese. Anyway, studying that night was no different than any other night. As usual, I cluttered my knowledge of Spanish and Portuguese into the mixing bowl of confusion.

About twenty minutes into my studying, I got another e-mail about the Airborne Hamster. Anxious to see
if there was a new video, I quickly opened the document.
Sure enough, as I looked at the message, the e-mail read,
"George Washington witnesses first American Airborne
Drop." There was a video attached, so I quickly opened
the media. As the video began playing, I could see the
same masked cadets were involved in this incident too.
Half were standing on the roof of Washington Hall, while
all the others were standing at the entrance to the mess
hall by a statue of George Washington. Similar to the
first video, the masked cadet on the roof threw the daring hamster from the roof while the guys on the ground
waited for the hamster's safe arrival. The only difference
between this video and the first was that they took the
time to add some heavy metal music to the tape. As my
roommates and I watched the video, we couldn't stop
laughing. The music really made a big difference in the
quality of the clip. With two successful jumps under her
belt, there was surely going to be a lot of buzz the next
morning during class. Quickly coming to the realization
that I had four tests the next day, I closed the video and
returned to the massive study session that was already
underway. I couldn't afford to waste another second
looking at such hogwash.

The next morning I was exhausted. I studied until 2:45 a.m. and really didn't sleep well because I was
worried about all the academic requirements. I was
concerned that I didn't study enough for all the tests.
Another difficult aspect of academics was the fact that
West Point taught classes using a thing called the Thayer
method. The name came from one of the first superin-
tendents in 1817. A man by the name Sylvanus Thayer
developed a way of teaching students to take tests first
and teachers to give lessons second. This method of instruction is still practiced almost 200 years later. One

might expect that taking tests on material that has never been taught proves to be an arduous task, but after a year or so, cadets become accustomed to the practice. The intent is to groom the cadets to learn how to teach themselves. My first experience with the Thayer method occurred on my first day of academics at West Point. There was no learning period or time to adapt to the concept; it was implemented from day one. Before showing up for my first day of class, I received e-mails from my instructors assigning homework and tests on the very first day. This was a shocking experience, coming from a typical high school class where instructors spoon-fed students information and gave weeks of notice before tests. Now, I was faced with an environment where not only did I have little notice, but I wasn't even being taught the material I was being tested on. The concept might sound ludicrous, but it really teaches students the importance of self-education and preparation for instruction. Education truly is a two-way street; most Americans think their academic failures are solely the part of their instructors. At West Point, they take this concept and flip it on its head. If you fail, it's because you poorly instructed yourself. You lacked the skills to prepare for professional instruction.

After a very long night of studying, my alarm rocked my tired body awake early in the morning. Following breakfast, I walked to my first class and consequently, my first test. I had a terrible feeling it wasn't going to be a good day. Even thinking about the Airborne Hamster couldn't lighten the mood. My American Politics test wasn't going to be easy, and there was a lot of information that I didn't even get a chance to study. Near the middle of the test, I knew I was a goner. There was no hope for my terrible performance on the test. Usually, I had a good sense of judgment for what the instructor might ask on the test, but not this time. I felt like I had studied the exact opposite subjects that were presented on the exam.

At the conclusion of the test, I decided to lick my wounds and drive on to the next exam. Immediately following the American Politics disaster was a Physics test. Although I didn't study for the test, I felt comfortable with the material. As I finished my final answers on the Physics exam, I felt like I passed. I was upset because I knew if I had more time to study, I would have performed much better on the graded requirement. If I didn't have to go to drill and march in circles for two hours yesterday, I know I would have performed better on the test.

With two graded requirements complete, I had one period off in order to prepare for the other two graded requirements and Engineering Math class. With the extra time, I studied more Portuguese because I knew it was going to be a difficult exam. There weren't many opportunities during the day to study, so cadets would always take advantage of the opportunity when it was available. The empty period went fast; if only class periods could go that fast, I used to think to myself. The next test that morning was Psychology. I had a feeling it was going to be harder than expected. It was a timed test, verbally given by the instructor. About halfway through the exam, I already knew I failed. There were twenty-five questions, and I already had ten blank answers. This was really going to be ugly. The format of the test totally threw me off guard. This was definitely an "F" performance and was going to have a catastrophic effect on my overall grade in the class.

As I stumbled to the mess hall for lunch, my friends could tell I was having a really difficult day. They tried to cheer me up by talking about the Airborne Hamster video, but nothing really lightened the mood. Talking about the humorous video actually started to make me even angrier. I couldn't understand how a person would have the time to make a funny video and endure all the classes and tests that I experienced on a daily basis. As they continued to talk about the hamster, I got so upset that I slammed my fists on the table and walked out during the middle of the meal. This obviously wasn't allowed, and if I got caught leaving the mess hall early, I would have received disciplined marching hours. I ran back to my room. Luckily, no one saw me return to my room to continue studying for the final test that afternoon. I studied even more Portuguese. The extra studying didn't even help because I couldn't stay focused on the material from being so upset with my scores earlier that morning. When my roommate, Jack, returned to the room after lunch, he didn't say a thing. He was beginning to understand my personality as well as he knew his own. At this point, not speaking was a better way of dealing with my frustration than discussing my problems. With little time left before my dreaded Portuguese exam, I slammed the door and ran to class.

When I got to class, some of the students were practicing different vocabulary words than I had studied.

I quickly asked, "Why are you guys practicing those words? They aren't on the test."

To my surprise, one of my friends insisted the test included a whole other page of vocabulary that I didn't study.

He said, "Preston, you needed to study page 343 too. If you look in the lesson outline, you'll see it's listed under the homework for today."

Sure enough, my friend was right. Hopefully those twenty words wouldn't be included on the test. As we took our seats and I prepared for the final test of the day, the teacher told us to take out a piece of paper and number the page from one to twenty-five. I was having flashbacks from the Psychology test. As the instructor gave the directions for the exam, I couldn't believe it was going to be another oral assessment. As the teacher began speaking completely in Portuguese, I quickly became confused and aggravated. Ten questions into the exam, he started asking vocabulary that I hadn't even studied. I knew it was from the page my friend warned me about. *How could I be so stupid to not look at the homework?* I became so focused on studying for the test that I neglected to study all the required material. After all my efforts and neglect for other subjects, I still failed the Portuguese test.

At the completion of the class, I stormed out of the room and headed to my final Engineering Math class. I couldn't think about anything but my poor performance for the day. Not even realizing that I had already walked to another building and was sitting in my Engineering Math class, it was obvious that my mind was in other places that afternoon.

This is the point in the day where my bad luck turned worse. As the second hand reached the top of the clock, the instructor quickly closed the door and directed the class to take out a pencil and a blank piece of paper. *He can't be serious*, I thought to myself. There is no way I was going to have tests in five classes all on the same day. Sure enough, the instructor started handing out a three-page quiz to everyone in the class.

"Today we are going to have a pop quiz on the required reading from last night," the instructor barked.

At this point, I thought about writing "Beat Navy" for each answer and turning it in. I was beyond frustrated and was aggravated by the fact that I had a graded requirement in every class. For the first and last time, I had doubts about my ability to graduate from the school. I remember this day as well as I remember graduation. It was the most discouraging day I ever experienced while attending West Point. For me, this was much worse than running twenty miles or not eating for a week straight. It was a mental fatality where I psychologically questioned my ability to endure the chaos of the esteemed institution. I failed the quiz. I was so overwhelmed I couldn't even talk or listen. At the conclusion of the quiz, the instructor began teaching the lesson for the quiz we just took.

During the middle of his lecture, I stood up and walked to the bathroom. For ten minutes, I stood in the bathroom and just looked in the mirror. As I looked at the dark circles around my eyes and my pale skin, my mind began running rampant. I couldn't handle the stress and all I wanted to do was scream.

Minutes later, I returned to the classroom and stared at the wall for the rest of the class. At this point, my body was going through the motions, but my mind was full of white noise. I didn't hear a thing for the rest of the class.

Later that evening, I laid on my bed and stared at the ceiling.

Jack, obviously knowing something was wrong, asked, "Preston, what's up, man?"

I didn't say anything. This was definitely out of my nature to ignore my best friend.

Jack could definitely sense something was wrong. After a few minutes, Jack continued.

"Look, this place will eat you alive only if you let it. If the planets aligned today, you can rest assured that it won't happen again for a while. Stay strong, bud."

Still not responding, I thought about Jack's advice. He was definitely right about the planets aligning. Having a graded requirement in five college-level classes was not common. As I pondered his advice even further, I realized I needed to stop feeling sorry for myself. Seeking pity wasn't going to fix my poor performance that day. The only thing that was going to fix my scores was continued hard work and dedication to my personal goals.

By the end of the night, Jack got me to start talking about the horrible experience. Talking about the terrible day really helped put my mind back on track. I slept well that night, and my mind was at ease, thanks to Jack.

The next morning, I woke up, feeling refreshed. It

was the start of a new day and new opportunities. When I opened my e-mail that morning, I saw yet another e-mail pertaining to the Airborne Hamster. Smiling and rolling my eyes, I clicked on the video that was attached. *What could these jokers have done now?* I thought to myself.

As the video began to play, I could see it was another video of the hamster conducting a jump. Like the second video, the creators incorporated music to enhance the clip. I was waiting to see what they did to upstage their previous two performances. Without much hesitation, the creators of the hamster videos exceeded all expectations once again. At the end of the jump, the video cut to one of the masked cadets' rooms. As the camera zoomed in on the furry little creature, it was standing on a desk when the song "The Ballad of the Green Berets" started playing. Then I could hear a voice over the music reading firm military orders for three awards that were being presented to the hamster. At this point, Jack and I watched the video with the biggest grins. The awards had even been miniaturized so they were proportional to the size of the little hamster. That little hamster had conducted herself with honor. Her chain of command was very proud as they placed her medals before her tiny little hamster feet. *What a circus!*

As the months progressed, I heeded Jack's advice and didn't let the Academy eat me alive. I stayed mentally strong and stopped feeling sorry for myself. Although that horrible day took a toll on my grades for the semester, I ended up getting all "A's" and "B's" in every class except Portuguese, in which I received a "C." I still speak Spanuguese to this day. We never saw another video of the Airborne Hamster. A couple years later, I heard who the suspected leader of the prank was. Needless to say, I wasn't surprised.

* * *

BLUF: Mental toughness is at the core of every leader and competitor, and it grooms them toward success.

The mind is an amazing thing. If a teacher asks a fourth-grade classroom of twenty children who thinks they could be the president of the United States, half the hands in the room would be raised. If the same question would be asked to twenty graduating high school seniors, the teacher would be laughed out of the room. What happened? Did the high school seniors realize the probability is 1 in 270 million, or did they loose their desire to always be the best due to lack of mental toughness?

As children become adults, a changing point occurs where they transition from being children who live in the moment to adults who discern the world that surrounds them. Oftentimes, the reality in which adults perceive the world around them is warped with a sense of limitation. I've found adults are like dogs inside an invisible fence. After only a couple days, dogs can be taught the boundaries with an electronic collar. In only a week, dogs can be trained to remain within their boundaries without even wearing a collar. Why did the dog stop trying to run outside the yard? Was it because he wasn't physically strong enough to endure the mild pain from the collar for a couple seconds? Or was the dog not mentally tough enough to continue trying? I would obviously argue the latter.

Most humans follow this same path of least resistance. They lack the mental toughness to continue trying, regardless of how many times they are denied access to their goals or aspirations. During my junior year at the Academy, we had Ross Perot as a guest lecturer. He was a very fascinating individual to hear. The most amazing part of his entire lecture was when he told us that he had applied to the Naval Academy five times before finally being admitted. Now he's a billionaire. I thought to my-self, *now here is a man with mental toughness!*

Mental toughness is something that is preached all across the country, but in reality, it is only practiced by few. The reason I remembered this terrible day over all the others was because this truly was the only day I actu-ally thought I couldn't make it. I've always held the be-lief that placing limitations on my potential would have a compounding effect. As a result of my own belief, my weak mind-set worried me. When a single limitation is set in place, it induces a mind-set that more limitations can follow. After a while, you've placed so many inhibi-tors in your life that you eventually give up on progress and goals and accept mediocrity for the rest of your life. Essentially, you become the dog trapped in the yard that continually gets smaller.

General Petraeus is probably one of the best living examples of mental toughness to graduate from West Point. He was the one General who emphatically believed that Iraq could be changed. Millions of people across the country wanted to take the path of least resistance and pull out of Iraq. He knew change was essential and capable. His mental toughness, combined with superior leadership, combated a massive insurgency that some might argue could have never been defeated based on historical examples. Instead of giving up and sitting in his symbolic yard, he kept attempting to break free until he shattered the perceived limitation. Here's a quick and admirable quote that General Petraeus said about mental toughness:

"Physical and mental toughness are essential to leadership. It's hard to lead from the front if you are in the rear of formation."

General David Petraeus

Director of the Central Intelligence Agency
Class of 1974, West Point
(Burton, 2008)

6

Units of Measure

"Cessna 1472, you are cleared for taxi to hold short line runway 09."

I couldn't believe it. I was sitting in the back of an airplane with my professor and classmate, ready to take flight. It was the start of my Cow year and my Aerospace Engineering classes were finally underway. I was so excited because for the first time, I was taking classes of my choosing. Even through high school, when other kids were taking electives, I was stuck taking Calculus and Advanced Chemistry in an effort to get into West Point. Additionally, once I got accepted and started attending college, West Point mandated a strict curriculum for the first two years. That was all behind me now because I was finally taking the classes that truly interested me. As a result, there I was, sitting in the back of a Cessna, getting ready to take flight.

My instructor, Major (MAJ) Patrick O'Brien, was an Apache Attack Helicopter pilot by trait and a West Point graduate from the class of 1991. Luckily, he taught almost all of my Aerospace Engineering classes and happened to be one of my favorite instructors. He was a great teacher, and I ultimately wanted to be an Apache helicopter pilot just like him. He had a unique ability to keep classes fun yet productive at all times.

That morning before the flight, I remember asking him what it was like flying a Cessna after spending so many hours in an attack helicopter.

The MAJ just laughed and said, "It's like driving a Corvette then having to trade it in for a Winnebago."

My classmate and I thought the comment was funny, but we weren't discouraged because we were very excited to get a ride in his Winnebago.

My classmate's name was Dan, and I could tell he was extremely excited. Prior to the flight, we had flipped a coin to see who would get to fly in the front seat with MAJ O'Brien. Unfortunately, he won. I was a little disappointed because I knew I should have picked heads.

"Ground Control, Cessna 1472 WILCO I'll call arrival short of runway 09," MAJ O'Brien answered back.

We didn't understand what the radio calls meant. All we wanted to do was start flying. The purpose of our flight was to get in the air and calculate the center of gravity on the aircraft. MAJ O'Brien was going to make a controlled input into the yoke and let the aircraft fix the condition. All the while, Dan and I would collect the data for the amount of fuel burned, change in elevation, and change in airspeed as it all corresponded to the change in time. Once we collected this information, we would have hours of crunching numbers to figure out the problems that were associated with the flight. Like all things at the Academy, we always paid our dues for having fun.

As MAJ O'Brien pulled the throttle back on the aircraft, the engine began to roar and we began to taxi. Our eyes lit up with anticipation.

MAJ O'Brien, not wasting any time to create excitement, said to Dan, "You want to taxi the aircraft to the runway?"

Dan, panting like a dog ready to get a treat, responded, "Absolutely, Sir!"

MAJ O'Brien, now looking at Dan, said, "All right. It's really simple. I'll control the power, so you don't have to worry about your speed. All I need you to do is take the yoke and steer this thing like you're driving a Ford Mustang."

That analogy hit well with Dan because both he and MAJ O'Brien owned a Mustang. Dan, eager and nervous at the same time, slowly began to lift his hands to the yoke. He had an enormous grin on his face, as he could feel the power of MAJ O'Brien's Winnebago of an aircraft. As we continued taxiing with Dan at the helm, he quickly became a little arrogant.

"Sir, this isn't real hard. I think you should let me take it off."

MAJ O'Brien, already anticipating Dan's question, said, "I'll make a deal with you, Dan. If you can get us safely to the runway, I'll let you take this baby off."

Dan, ecstatic at this point, knew that wasn't going to be a problem. How hard could it possibly be to taxi a little Cessna to the end of the runway? It was a sure bet, and he was going to have huge bragging rights back in the classroom when everyone heard that MAJ O'Brien had let him conduct a takeoff. From the back seat, I had a bird's eye view of the two pilot's stations. It was like watching a sixteen year old who just got his license drive for the first time.

As Dan's first of many turns approached, MAJ O'Brien kept his feet firmly on the pedals and his hand on the throttle. He was looking out the left window as if he was not even paying any attention to Dan's first turn. Dan, on the other hand, had his tongue pushed out the right side of his lips and couldn't take his eyes off the yellow line that ran directly down the middle of the taxiway. Dan had such a death grip on the yoke that I could see his hands turning white. As he executed the first turn perfectly, MAJ O'Brien was still looking out the left side of the window like nothing had even happened.

Dan, marveling at his own perfectly executed turn, said to MAJ O'Brien, "Sir, did you see how that center wheel never came off the yellow line?"

MAJ O'Brien, appearing to wake up from a trance, said to Dan, "No, I missed that. I'll pay close attention to your next one."

As we continued down the taxiway and prepared for the next turn, Dan said, "All right, Sir. Make sure you pay attention this time."

MAJ O'Brien, nodding his head, said, "OK, let's see it."

This time as Dan began turning the yoke to the left, I could see the aircraft was slowly veering off the line and over to the far right side of the taxiway. Abruptly, Dan began turning the yoke even harder to the left to correct the problem.

As the aircraft slowly worked its way back over to the yellow line, MAJ O'Brien commented, "Dan, you nearly ran us into the grass. Are you sure you even have a license?"

Dan, very embarrassed and confused, said, "Sir, I think there's something wrong with the steering on the aircraft."

MAJ O'Brien, nodding his head in concern, said to Dan, "I'll be glad to take it off your hands and taxi the aircraft the rest of the way."

Understanding the implications of the Major's request, Dan quickly responded, "Sir, that won't be necessary. I'm sure the steering is fine. That last turn was my fault."

At this point, Dan would rather have crashed the aircraft into the runway lights than miss the unique opportunity to take off. As we continued down the long stretch of taxiway, MAJ O'Brien began looking out the left window again. Not paying attention to Dan's taxiing, the aircraft started drifting to the right of the centerline. Dan, hoping that MAJ O'Brien hadn't seen the mistake, quickly applied a lot of left yoke to correct for the error.

As the aircraft quickly corrected itself, Dan gripped the yoke even tighter. MAJ O'Brien, looking clueless, was still staring at something out the left side of the aircraft. Dan was able to keep the aircraft on the yellow line for a few seconds, then it began to drift to the right once again. Dan, getting more worried, quickly corrected the mistake with a left yoke and brought the aircraft back to the centerline. As we got closer to the "T" intersection where Dan needed to make a ninety-degree turn, MAJ O'Brien brought his attention back inside the aircraft.

He said, "All right, Dan, here's the final turn. You can see the runway out your right door."

"Roger, Sir. This turn will be much better than the last," Dan remarked.

As we approached the "T" intersection, Dan slowly started turning the yoke to the right. As the aircraft continued straight, Dan applied even more right yoke. Still nothing was happening and you could tell that he was getting concerned.

"Turn right any day, Dan," MAJ O'Brien remarked.

Then out of nowhere, the aircraft made a hard abrupt turn to the left.

Dan started screaming, "Sir, the controls are reversed, the controls are reversed!"

At this point, the aircraft had turned left at the "T" intersection, which was the opposite direction the aircraft needed to go in order to get on the runway.

Dan, scared out of his mind, said, "Sir, take the controls...take the controls."

MAJ O'Brien, laughing hysterically, looked at Dan and said, "Take it easy, I've had the controls the whole time."

Pausing to stare at Dan with a look of amazement and disappointment at the same time, MAJ O'Brien said, "Dan, you taxi an aircraft with your feet!"

Realizing that he had been duped by the astute and

hilarious MAJ O'Brien, Dan hung his head in shame. Instead of telling the glorious story of how he took the Cessna off, he was now going to be ridiculed by all our classmates for not knowing the aircraft is taxied with the foot pedals.

My Cow year was interesting because duties as a cadet became much easier, yet academics became more difficult. All my Engineering classes were very interesting and challenging at the same time. Although West Point was the first engineering school in America, many cadets don't actually major in Engineering. My expectation upon acceptance to the school was that at least half the students would either major in Electrical, Mechanical, or Civil Engineering. In actuality, only ten percent of all students majored in these fields of study. The Engineering Department was notorious for having the hardest classes at the Academy, and as a result, many cadets opt out of making the experience any harder than it already was. It was usually easy to pick out Engineering students because they were the ones in their rooms studying on Saturday nights.

For three years I lived with two other Engineering students. I lived with Jack for my last three years, and along the way we picked up another guy by the name of Mac Davis. A room that contained three Engineering students helped alleviate the animosity toward other friends who didn't study nearly as hard. We would often be walking back to our room from the bathroom and see our classmates going out for the night or doing anything other than studying. The three of us, on the other hand, were stuck in the barracks, working through problems every night. I feel like I know Mac and Jack as well as I know myself; we would do anything for each other.

Mac was a unique individual. He was one of the smartest guys I knew at the Academy. He had an ability to take what the common world sees as normal and flip it upside down. After he could stand something on its head, he then had the ability to convince anyone that this is now the standard. He was a remarkable roommate, because anytime I didn't understand an Engineering problem, he would quickly know the answer. It was like having the professor as a roommate. At times, he could actually explain things better than the professors in class. Jack and I would look like big dummies as we would scratch our heads in confusion to most of the problems we encountered each night.

That academic year, Mac and I had a class together called Fluid Dynamics. Essentially, the class studied the behavior of fluids and its characteristics through different mediums. The fluid could be water, oil, or even air. Halfway through the class, our instructor developed a project in which we needed to calculate the terminal velocity of a toy soldier on a parachute. We were going to calculate the velocity based on the measurements of the chute and the weight of the toy and make a prediction. Once the prediction was calculated, we would then test our numbers by throwing the toy off buildings or any other location of our choosing. The instructor allowed us to work in teams. As a result, Mac and I teamed up together to tackle the fun little project. Living together, for this tasking, was going to make the coordination a breeze. After the instructor handed out the packets describing the details of the project, all the students began reading the thorough instructions.

The packet read, "75% of your grade will be taken from the briefing given at the end of the project." I made sure to highlight that important note. Mac, reading through the packet at lightning speed, raised his hand in reference to a quandary he had uncovered.

"Yes, Mac. What's your question?" The instructor commented.

Mac, not missing any details, said, "Sir, I see you

didn't specify the units that you want the final answer to be presented with."

At the Academy, details like this were very specific. Instructors would always want the students to present the answers with the same units, such as feet per second. The instructor was clearly surprised that he had forgotten such an important detail. He grabbed Mac's packet and started flipping through the pages and looking for the missing piece of information. After a minute or two, the instructor clearly realized that the important detail had been omitted.

As a result, the instructor said, "All right, I made a mistake. You guys can use any units you'd like."

Everyone in the class, still looking at their packets, nodded their heads in understanding. Mac just looked at me with a smirk and eyes that read, "How'd you like that, Preston?" I just looked back and rolled my eyes. This was Mac; he was so quick-witted and observant. I would often see him make fun of friends and they didn't even realize anything had happened. He clearly thought on a different level than anyone else.

A couple days later, Mac and I began work on the parachute project.

"Preston, could you come over here and look at this thing I got on my computer?" Mac said.

As I took a break from the Thermodynamics home-work I was working on, I walked over to his desk. As I got closer and looked at his screen, I could see that he had completed the entire project. On his computer, he had created a program that allowed the user to change the input numbers and automatically recalculate the en-tire problem. He had a look on his face that said, "That couldn't have been any easier." Feeling very guilty for not helping him out with all the calculations, I quickly volunteered to put the PowerPoint presentation together in order to brief our findings.

Later that evening, I spent a couple of hours putting our presentation together with all the math formulas and calculations that Mac had figured out so quickly. While typing, I heard three knocks at the door. This could only mean one thing: we had a plebe at the door.

Jack, anxious to take a break from his Civil Engineering homework, quickly shouted, "Come in."

As the door flew open, we all looked at the plebe who was standing at attention in the entrance of our room.

The Plebe, with his eyes practically popping out of his head, said, "Gentlemen, excuse me. I knocked on the wrong door."

Jack, feasting on the opportunity, said, "Oh, I'm so sorry to hear that. What room where you trying to find?"

The plebe, stuttering at this point, said, "Sir, I was trying to go to Cadet Private Spencer's room."

On average, we would see a plebe accidentally knock on an upperclassman's door about once or twice a semester. I know when I was a plebe I did it at least twice. Many of the buildings had multiple levels, and if you were not paying close attention, you could sometimes get confused and go to the wrong room. If and when it happened, the upper class was always ready to strike.

"Spencer, huh?" Jack replied.

The plebe, clearly realizing that Jack was baiting him, prepared for the worst. It was then that all three of us stood up from our chairs and began slowly walking toward the plebe who was still standing at the entrance to the door. As we made our predatory steps closer, the plebe took a chance at luck.

"Gentlemen, I greatly apologize for the inconvenience. Would you like me to close the door behind me?" he said.

"What...are you serious?" Jack said. "You mean you don't want to stay and chat with us?"

Realizing the question had negative implications either way it was answered, the plebe said, "Respectfully, gentlemen, I would like to get to Private Spencer's room."

Jack quickly shouted, "Fourth Class, do you normally ignore direct questions from upperclassmen? That was a yes or no question."

The plebe, realizing that he wasn't leaving anytime soon, avoided the sweet talk and went right into survival mode.

"No, Sir," he responded.

"OK, then answer my question. Do you want to stay and chat with us?" Mac asked again.

Typically, this scenario would play out in one of two ways. The plebe would say yes and endure the countless questions of knowledge, which we considered chatting. This would typically take about thirty minutes of his time. The second scenario involved him saying no, and then we would get upset and question his intentions for coming to our room. Eventually, this would lead back to the same countless questions of knowledge that would take thirty minutes of his time. As we anxiously anticipated the plebe's reaction, we were all astounded with his response.

"Gentlemen, to answer your question honestly, I'd have to say no. The fact of the matter is I thought I was on the fourth floor when in fact I was on the third. The last thing I wanted to do was knock on your door because that is an obvious recipe for disaster. Based on the fact that your books are open, I surmise you probably have a lot of studying to do tonight. The last thing I want to do is take up any more of your time."

Mac, loving the honesty and creative response, said, "All right, Fourth Class, beat it. Next time read the name tapes on the door."

The Plebe, obviously surprised that his creative answer actually worked, conducted an about face and sprinted away.

As we closed the door and got back in our seats, Jack

looked at the wall and said, "Mac, you're never handling the issues of this room ever again."

Mac, laughing at Jack's comment, said, "OK, Jack. Next time I'll put on the baboon routine that you and Preston have so flawlessly mastered."

The night before the parachute project was due, I put the final touches on our briefing in order to ensure the aesthetics were pleasing to the instructor's eyes.

Before finishing up, Mac said, "Hey Preston, could you send me the presentation when you're done? I want to add a few things."

Not thinking anything of his request, I replied, "Sure, no problem."

Minutes later, the presentation was complete and ready for Mac's review. With a quick e-mail, it was now out of my hands and back with its creator. Later in the evening as I was sitting at my desk and working on some history homework, Mac got out of his chair and stood by the door. As I looked over to see what he was doing, I could see that he had a tape measure. For some reason, Mac was trying to wedge it between the top of the door jam.

Looking at Mac in disbelief, Jack said, "Mac, you didn't get any taller since last week. Why are you measuring your height?"

Mac, very sensitive about his height, didn't hesitate in saying, "No, I'm trying to measure your ego over here. The only problem is, I don't think this ten-foot measuring tape is big enough."

Admiring Mac's quick wit and satire, Jack and I laughed and went back to studying while Mac continued with his bizarre project.

The next day, Mac and I sat down in our Fluids class and had everything ready to brief. I think we were the third group to present. It was nice not going first, because we could learn from the mistakes of the early presenters.

After the first group was finished with their presentation, I saw that our answer was really close to the same thing they had computed. The speed we calculated was 2.5 feet per second and the group that just finished estimated 2.6 feet per second. This was always a good sign when other teams were coming up with the same numbers. Mac's quick math sure didn't hinder his ability to calculate the right information.

As the second group gave their presentation, I could clearly tell they weren't even close.

During the briefing, Mac leaned over to my desk and whispered, "Hey, you take all the slides at the beginning and I'll take the last two. I'll brief the answer and take all the questions."

Looking back and nodding in approval, I knew this was probably the smart decision, considering Mac could sell the instructor on our answer even if it was wrong.

As the second group quickly finished their terrible presentation, Mac and I soon found ourselves at the front of the class. The briefing started off well, and it appeared the instructor liked the layout of our presentation. After my portion of the brief, it was now time to turn the presentation over to Mac. After a short introduction, Mac flipped to the last slide and began to brief.

As I looked at the screen, I had to rub my eyes to be sure I wasn't seeing things. To my surprise, all the numbers were completely different than what I had seen the night prior in our room. As I marveled at Mac's ability to brief all the changes on a whim, I began to notice that all the changes were intentional. Evidently, Mac changed all the numbers after I was done with the slides last night and didn't even tell me what was going on. My smile quickly turned to a frown. Furious that he wouldn't have included me on the changes, I watched with an attitude clearly displayed on my face. Nearing the end of the brief, Mac clicked the remote and advanced the presentation to the last slide. As the final piece of data was displayed on the board, one object was present. It was the final answer and the numbers were completely different than our original conclusion. I read the answer to myself at the same time Mac read it out loud to the class.

I read, ".448 MACs per second."

What the heck is a MAC, I thought to myself? Not only did we miss the answer to the question, but we didn't even give the answer in real units. That would be the equivalent of saying, *I traveled a distance of ten degrees Celsius down the road today.* It didn't make any sense. To make the situation even more upsetting, Mac had a big grin on his face as if the whole thing was funny. As the presentation concluded, Mac asked the class if anyone had any questions.

Not hesitating, the instructor said, "Mac, please tell me, what in the world is a MAC?"

Pausing briefly and looking at the floor, Mac responded, "Sir, that is my height."

Grabbing my forehead and shaking my head, I couldn't believe what I just heard. *His height was the unit of measure that he used to calculate the terminal velocity of the parachute toy?* At this point every guy in the class erupted with laughter.

The instructor, smiling and laughing at the same time, said, "Mac, why did you use your height as a measurement of distance?"

Taking his time, Mac replied, "Sir, last week when I asked what units you wanted the answer in, you said to use anything we wanted. As a result, I really didn't care for the metric or English unit system, so I created my own."

The professor, absolutely loving Mac's creativity, said, "Mac, I'm going to need a conversion table to convert your answer."

Mac quickly responded, "Sir, there are 5.583 feet per every MAC."

As the class was barely able to hold their laughter to-

gether, they all watched the instructor pull out a calcula-
tor and convert the .448MAC/second to 2.5 feet/second.

Happy with the conversion, the instructor said, "Very
good. Your answer is exactly what I was looking for. This
was an "A" presentation, but I'm going give you an "A+"
for the creative effort and satire."

Mac and I were grinning from ear to ear as we walked
away. When we got back to our seats, I looked over at
Mac.

He said, "I should have let you brief that last part."

I just laughed with joy as Mac and I enjoyed the "A+"
that we earned that day.

* * *

The BLUF of this story is creative thinking drastically increases the potential and productivity of any organization. Additionally, the individual responsible for
the unique idea(s) gains the respect and admiration from
superiors, peers, and subordinates alike.

George S. Patton once said, "If everybody is thinking
alike, then somebody isn't thinking."

I'm sure everyone has worked in an ad hoc group
and noticed the different personalities within the faction.
The organization will always include the freeloaders who
really don't do anything but take up the oxygen in the
room. Then there are the worker bees who will help the
group succeed but lack the ability to make decisions on
their own. They typically wait for the leader to tell them
what to do. Once they have direction, they'll complete
the tasks assigned, but nothing more. Then occasionally,
a couple of leaders will emerge from the group. Typically,
these are people who have the ability to think outside the
box and task the others with duties and responsibilities.
Good leaders can take an existing plan and execute it,

while excellent leaders can take an existing plan, improve the fundamentals through creativity, and then execute it with better profitability or results than the original concept.

Be wary of the individual who makes comments like, "We already tried that" or "It would take too long." These are the comments and ideas of the followers. They have a tendency to be inhibitors to the potential of creative thinking. The idea is to stretch one's imagination and the possibilities while refraining from limited aptitude. Creative thinking doesn't necessarily involve big ideas or big concepts. Small amounts of creative thinking can collectively improve the fertility of the group and dramatically boost one's morale and reputation.

Although the story provided funny examples of creative thinking, the foundation is the key point to twig. Strong leaders never focus on the way things have always been, but instead, focus on the way things could be improved to benefit the welfare of the people they lead. They use a tool called critical reasoning. This is a systematic technique used to kindle critical thinking. One must analyze the task, identify goal(s), and clarify the problem that needs to be solved. Although critical reasoning requires many other aspects, this basic outline is a starting point for leaders to build upon. Many resources are available for further research on this topic in order to develop one's creative thinking skills.

Despite Admiral Mullen's alma mater, below is a great example of how the Chairman of the Joint Chiefs of Staff views the importance of the topic that has been highlighted in this chapter.

"The only constant will be change," Mullen said. "Military recruiting, education, training, promotions and retention will all change to meet the new realities of the 21st century," he said.

"All of this is driven by the increase in the speed of war. We are up against a quick and adaptive enemy," the chairman said. "We're not going to win until we get ahead of the enemy, and that takes some creative thinking. We've made a lot of progress, but we've got a long way to go."

Admiral Michael Mullen
Chairman of the Joint Chiefs of Staff
Class of 1968, United States Naval Academy
(Garamone, 2008)

Mac Davis and I

7

A Christmas Story

There once was a baby elephant that was tied to a small wooden stake early in its life. The elephant was so little and weak that it couldn't possibly pull the stake from the ground no matter how hard it tried. The little elephant was being cared for with food and water, but the owner knew that over time, the elephant would give up and not understand its true capabilities of escaping. As the early months progressed, the baby elephant would attempt fewer times a day to pull the small wooden stake from the ground. The animal eventually came to grips with a false reality that the wooden stake prevented any of his movement. Years later, as the massive creature possessed insurmountable strength and the ability to move even the homes of his captors, it still sat next to the small wooden stake. The obtuse animal had grown to believe in a false reality that its movement was restricted. Even more importantly, the animal didn't understand its capability and potential. What would happen if this animal was miraculously endowed with the knowledge of its strength? Would it seek retribution for the jaded life that the owner had imparted over all the years? This next story will answer those questions, among others, as we explore the notorious Christmas dinner.

It was the middle of December and I was a Cow at the Academy. I held the duty of being a platoon sergeant for the semester. For anyone who has seen a military movie, a platoon sergeant is generally the instructor who's constantly training the soldiers and possesses the demeanor of a drill sergeant. It was a fun job and I definitely learned a lot about my responsibilities as a future leader.

There was always a lot of anticipation during this time of year because Christmas break was getting close. For most of the plebes, they hadn't been home since graduating from high school. With the end of the first semester looming, many cadets were stressed from studying for academic finals. The fear of failing a course and needing to attend the Summer Training Academic Period (STAP) was more than enough motivation to pass one's classes. I heard stories from friends who had actually attended STAP, and they said it was terrible knowing that the only three weeks of leave you get a year was spent attending the one course they had failed. For eight hours a day, six days a week, they would relearn all the material taught for that class during an entire semester. Most guys weren't ashamed of attending STAP because it wasn't like anyone thought that passing these classes was easy. In fact, anytime a person would attend STAP, they would commonly refer to them as a STAP Ranger. The name was pulled from the elite Army Special Forces unit commonly referred to as the U.S. Army Rangers. We always had a tendency to reverse the meaning of everything.

With the thought of STAP always in the back of our minds, cadets would proceed cautiously into the term-end examination (TEE) week. This is simply called "finals" by the rest of the world. When I first became a cadet, I thought the school purposely came up with acronyms for everything just so no one would understand anything we were talking about. For instance, a test was called a written partial review (WPR), while a briefing was called an intermediate partial review (IPR). There were three-letter words for anything and everything. In an attempt to motivate the upper class during TEE week, it was mandatory for the plebes to greet any upperclassman with the saying, "Beat the Dean, Sir." This phrase was in reference to beating the Dean of the academic board.

When I would walk to class during TEE week, it felt like every fourth person would utter the message, "Beat the Dean, Sir."

Some upperclassman would respond back, "Yeah, beat him with a stick," while others just looked at the ground in utter concentration while they walked to their next test.

That night, I was on my way back from the library when I passed one of the Firsties correcting some plebes in the hall. The name of the Firstie was Christopher Dean. Dean came from a family of military heroes. His father once came to our school and talked to our company about combat operations. He had earned two silver stars and multiple purple hearts as a Green Beret Special Forces Commander in Vietnam. We often joked with Chris, saying he had pretty big boots to fill, considering his father retired as a full-bird Colonel, just one rank below General. The one thing that was most memorable about Chris was the fact that he looked so young. He had what most people commonly refer to as a baby face. If there was one person who could pass as his twin, it would be the character "Ralphie" from the movie "A Christmas Story." Despite his adolescent looks, Dean was ferocious when it came to dealing with plebes. I loved to watch him get his hands on some of the biggest Plebe football players and work his magic. He looked like a chihuahua picking a fight with a caged pit bull. As I got closer to Dean, who was really putting on a production that night, I could begin to hear the one-way conversation he was having with the fourth class.

"Who made this picture?" Dean shouted, holding up a piece of paper that had evidently been printed from someone's computer. "I swear to God, every one of you bean-heads are going to stand outside my room for the rest of the night until I get some answers," he continued.

As I got closer, I saw he was holding a small poster from the movie "A Christmas Story." Evidently, someone had superimposed Dean's head over the picture of the character Ralphie and then hung it on his door. Delaying the walk back to my room at this point, because I was really curious to see how things were going to play out, three more plebes walked down the hall and greeted Dean.

As the plebes passed, they proceeded with the mandatory greeting, "Beat the Dean, Sir!"

This was like watching an atom bomb explode for the first time.

Chris began screaming, "NO...NO...NO. Listen, the last thing you are going to beat is the Dean! I'm the Dean! If there's one person at this institution that you won't beat, it's me!"

The poor plebes couldn't have chosen a worse time to pass by Chris. Furious, Chris said, "You three stand by the wall with these other delinquents."

As I stood there trying to keep a straight face while looking at the six plebes in front of Chris, he continued.

"All right, whoever's responsible for making this picture, hold your fist out so I don't have to hear your squeaky little pathetic voice."

Evidently, Chris got word that the picture was hung by one of the original three plebes who were standing outside his room.

Before he could finish his sentence, two of the plebes had stuck out their fists at the same exact time, claiming responsibility for the poster. We called this "jumping on the grenade" when two guys are ready to take the blame for something that potentially neither of them had committed.

"Oh, really...," Dean slowly said. "So this picture was

miraculously printed from two inkjets at the same time? Wow. SGT Pysh, can you believe that?" Dean said as he looked at me in confusion.

Trying not to steal his show, yet at the same time playing into his hand, I said, "That doesn't seem to make any sense; one picture yet two printers."

As silence set in, Dean just waited for one of them to speak. It was a long awkward pause.

"Sir, can I ask a question?" the one plebe who had his hand out said.

Dean, replying almost instantaneously, said, "You just did, numbnuts. I guess you should have asked for two questions."

The immediate reply was then followed by more awkward silence.

Chris was quick on his feet and would often come back with questions to questions, causing confusion and a sense of being outwitted. Not giving the plebe a chance to ask his real inquiry, Dean continued.

"You guys want to play games? I love games. Since you guys like the movie "A Christmas Story" so much, I want you to write me a theme. Before breakfast formation tomorrow, I want a three-page paper on what you want for Christmas."

Humiliated and frustrated, this was the last thing the plebes needed while studying for their final exams.

After the plebes left, Chris looked at me and said, "If they have enough time to make stupid pictures of me, I guess they'll have enough time to write a stupid essay."

The next morning at breakfast, Chris abruptly stopped by my table and said, "Do you know what those little bastards wrote that they wanted for Christmas?"

Slowly looking up from my meal, I said, "A Red Ryder BB Gun?"

Stunned, Chris said, "How'd you know."

Taking my time, I said, "Chris, come on. You were a

plebe. What would you have written?"

Chris, not taking any time to think, responded, "Yeah, you're right."

Without hesitation, he headed out in the direction of where the three plebes were eating breakfast. I'm pretty sure that wasn't the end of that whole fiasco. He definitely wouldn't have let that slide.

The building where we were having breakfast that morning, and every morning for that matter, was called Washington Hall. This is a massive building that houses the 4,000-plus seats where the cadets eat every single meal. The ceiling is four stories high and the large stone walls have stained-glass windows. The inside has medieval architecture that makes one feel like they're stepping back into 15th century Britain. The mess hall is broken down into six wings, which all meet at a focal point in the middle. From an aerial perspective it would look like a wheel with spokes, with each spoke being a wing with more than six hundred seats. The structure is massive and the thousands of cadets are dwarfed by the colossal walls and ceiling. The next time you go to McDonald's and see an eight-person team frantically working behind the counter to make four Happy Meals, imagine the preparations needed to feed the four thousand angry cadets who, having finished an enthralling morning of academics, are ready to eat — now. This is the scenario three times a day throughout the entire year.

Outside, before every meal, the senior cadets take accountability of the entire school in a matter of minutes. After this is complete, all the cadets march into the mess hall. The students funnel through nine large doors in a neat and orderly fashion; the whole process typically takes place within five minutes. Anxiously waiting to eat, they stand in front of their seats until instructed to sit down. The command to "Take seats" is given at a location in the middle of the mess called the "Poop Deck." Once everyone is assembled inside, a member of the senior class goes to the third story of the Poop Deck and calls the huge room to attention. At the drop of a dime, there is utter silence throughout the entire hall. Everyone is quiet and listens for the command "Take seats." Once that command is echoed throughout the hall, everyone simultaneously pulls out their chairs and sits down. It's quite a sight to see the efficiency and effectiveness of the whole operation.

As a whole, December was a great month at the Academy. It started off with the Army vs. Navy football game and ended with Christmas break. With so much happening, there was still only one event that stood out in my memory more than anything else: Christmas Dinner.

Every year on the Thursday before Christmas break, the school would have a Christmas dinner at the mess hall. This was one of the few times that the school really pulled out all the stops. They served a wonderful turkey dinner with stuffing, mashed potatoes, eggnog, and anything else you would see at Grandma's house. They had a jazz band playing Christmas music and everyone was dressed in the most formal uniform they had. This was the one and only night that the upper class actually embraced the plebes and treated them like family.

In order to prepare for the Christmas Dinner, the plebes had the very important job of decorating each table in the mess hall. Like everything at the Academy, this became an intense competition among the thousands of upperclassmen. Every table had exactly ten seats and an even distribution of class rank per table. Therefore, one would typically see approximately two to three Firsties, Cows, Yearlings, and plebes per table. The Firstie who was in charge of each table was called the "Table Commandant." He would stack the table with his favorite upper-class friends and then the plebes would circulate among the tables every month or so. Normally, the

Table Commandant would never swap out his upper-class friends who sat at his table. Like anything else, this created a situation for the plebes in which some tables were more challenging than others. I happened to be sitting at one of the tables that was considered to be more challenging. As a result, our Table Commandant, Todd Cody, expected the plebes to really decorate the table to perfection. He wanted Christmas decorations on every inch of the table. Todd wasn't about to be outperformed by Chris Dean's table, which was rumored to be making Christmas gifts mandatory for all upperclassmen. Todd's uncle was a Four-Star General and the Vice Chief of Staff of the whole Army, so we used to tease the hell out of him for that. Todd was a cadet Battalion Commander, which meant that he was in charge of approximately 500 cadets during his senior year. The last thing the plebes wanted to do was make him angry.

The day of the big dinner was upon us. All morning, cadets had been anticipating the fun-filled evening to come. Constant reminders were given to the plebes that our table better be decorated better than any other. Todd's best friend, Nick Ryan, who was also a Firstie, was adamant about the plebes' ability to prep the table for the night's festivities.

"If you little smackers want to eat during second semester, you better outperform CDT Dean's table tonight. I refuse to have the Dean beat me during TEE week," Ryan said.

He was obviously playing on the whole "Beat the Dean" adage. The plebes were nodding their heads in agreement and smirking at the joke.

They said "Yes, Sir" in unison.

Nick told me that when he was a plebe, he had a wonderful time enduring all the jokes referring to him as "Private Ryan." As luck would have it, the blockbuster movie "Saving Private Ryan" came out the same summer that Nick was going through Beast Barracks. One can only image the amount of harassment that induced.

"Save me, Private Ryan. Save me!" the upper class would scream as they passed him walking down the hall.

That night as we attended dinner formation, anticipation was running rampant. The upper class couldn't wait to see how well the fourth class had decorated the tables. The plebes from our table had a look on their faces like they had been outperformed. As Todd gave the command to march to the mess hall, a buzz of excitement filled the formation. We marched up the steps and through the large wooden doors and looked inside the winter wonderland that the plebes had turned Washington Hall into that night.

The jazz band was playing "Jingle Bells" and the massive room began to fill with Christmas cheer. As we approached our table, a few hundred feet into the building, we could see that the plebes had covered the entire table with wrapping paper. In the middle was a small Christmas tree that had small gifts with all the upperclassmen's names on them. By the look on Todd and Nick's faces, they were pleased with what the fourth class had done.

Todd, shaking his head, said, "Good job tonight. I can tell you guys put a lot of time into the decorations."

This type of sincerity wasn't shown toward the fourth class very often, and you could tell they appreciated the comment. Just as Todd had finished his remark to the plebes, a deafening and obnoxious roar of ringing Christmas bells was heard.

Two tables down, Chris Dean's plebes were holding an enormous sound system, blasting the theme from the movie "A Christmas Story." Standing on top of a chair and completely stoked, Dean started to scream.

"Nobody beats the Dean, baby. Nobody!"

As we took a closer look at his table, the plebes had actually set up an electric train around the outside of the table. In the middle was a real tree that the plebes must have chopped down and drug a couple of miles to the mess hall. Despite the fact that Dean had beaten everyone else's table, Todd and Nick couldn't help but smile and laugh at Chris. Everyone knew the night was only going to get crazier.

Then very abruptly, we heard the announcement "Brigade, attention."

Tonight, it took a couple extra seconds to calm everyone down when we heard the announcement from the Poop Deck. All the excitement of finishing classes, going home for break, and the decorations caused everyone to forget about their military requirements. This type of thing never happened.

The meal was absolutely delicious. I couldn't believe the cooks could make so many servings and still keep the integrity of a home-cooked meal. Near the end of the feast, the plebes stood up and began pulling the small presents out of the tree. As they handed out each gift in rank order, Todd told the Yearlings to open theirs first. As the two Yearlings began to unwrap their gifts, I could see they got something in a pink box. As the final pieces of tape were removed, we could see the plebes had bought the two male Yearlings a box of tampons. The Yearlings were trying to act upset, but they gave up halfway through their spiel and just started laughing. It was beautiful; I could only imagine what we were preparing to unwrap.

Todd, laughing hysterically at this point, said, "All right, Cows, you're up next."

Meanwhile, we could see the plebes over at Dean's table were beginning to hand out their gifts. Needless to say, we hurried up so we could watch the comedy show that was about to ensue at his table.

Slightly disappointed because we all received the same package, we angrily opened our gift together. Beneath the horribly wrapped present was a box that read,

"The Pamela Ramherson Love Doll." We couldn't believe it; these crazy plebes had bought us a blow-up doll.

Todd, barely able to hold his laughter together, said, "Someone start blowing that up and put it under the table."

As the Firsties started unwrapping their small gifts, it was clear the plebes knew which side their bread was buttered on. They bought Todd and Nick their two favorite movies.

As soon as all the gifts were opened, Todd quickly gave the command to head over to Dean's table to see what the plebes had purchased. Getting there just in time, we heard one of the plebes make an announcement to Dean.

"Sir, we think Santa forgot to bring your gift to dinner tonight."

Dean, laughing but grinning at the same time, shouted back, "Oh, yeah? Well, I think Santa forgot to give you a sense of humor."

The plebe, slightly rolling his eyes, didn't waste any time when he reached under the table and pulled out Dean's gift.

By the shape of the long, slender box, it could only be one thing. Chris began sliding the wrapping paper off the box as all the tables were intently watching him open his gift.

It was then that I heard someone shout, "They got him a Red Ryder BB Gun!"

Half the wing erupted into laughter as Dean, absolutely loving the gift, pulled it out of the box and held it over his head like an award. As he held the new gun in the air, the crowd of people all cheered and laughed. The ruckus was so loud that everyone else in the wing actually quieted down in an effort to see what provoked the noise. The cadets continued to get more rowdy as the dinner progressed, and this is when things went from bad to worse.

Shortly after Chris got his beloved Red Ryder carbine air rifle with a compass in the stock, it was time to conduct the traditional singing of "The Twelve Days of Christmas." I'm not sure how far back this tradition goes, but over the past couple years, cadets have gotten into a bad habit of lifting up tables and chairs during the song. To organize the event, one of the Firsties sent out an e-mail breaking down the tables into twelve different sections. Each section would sing one verse of the song. Like all things at West Point, even singing the song turned into a competition.

Near the end of the meal, one of the Firsties climbed to the top of the Poop Deck and made an announcement.

"Attention all cadets. We are now going to sing 'The Twelve Days of Christmas.' Be advised you are not allowed to pick up tables or chairs through the duration of the song."

As a little old lady sat down at a piano that was hooked up to all the speakers throughout the massive hall, cadets began looking around. The cadets looked like young kids who were trying to locate their parents in order to avoid punishment for the transgressions they were about to commit. As the first verse of the song began, we could hear a group of cadets from the south wing begin singing.

"On the first day of Christmas my true love gave to me..."

This is where things started to get out of control. As the song continued, we could see cadets start to lift their large tables in the air and over their heads when it was their turn to sing. No one seemed very worried about getting in trouble, considering there was only one Army officer on duty that night to control the discipline of the entire mess hall. To make things even more complex, the cadets were only lifting the tables in the air when it was their turn to sing. In an attempt to stop the madness, the officer in charge that night would frantically run in the direction of where the tables were being lifted. The only problem was, once he got near the delinquents, their tables would be back on the ground before he could identify who was responsible.

Dean, as fearless as if leading the charge against enemy combatants, had no problem taking the charade to the next level. As it came to our verse, "five golden rings," Dean actually got on top of the table as the group of underclassmen hoisted him into the air. Standing on top of the table with his arms out, invoking applause, Dean didn't have a fear in the world. The 600 cadets standing in our wing knew the game had been taken to the next level.

As the song finished its ninth round, it began again with "ten lords a leaping." Dean, quickly gathering more troops to prepare for the "five golden rings" verse, started stacking chairs on top of the table. Dean had expected others in the wing would try the same stunt during the next round and he wasn't about to be outdone. Nick, seeing the direction Dean was heading, grabbed the blow-up doll underneath our table and ran it over to Dean while he was starting his climb to the top of the chairs that were stacked on top of the table. Some might say that this is the point where the elephant officially pulled the wooden stake out of the ground. As the 300 cadets in our section sang the drawn-out "five golden rings," Dean had once again topped any meager attempt of his competitors.

Fifteen feet in the air with a Red Ryder BB Gun in one hand and a Pamela Ramherson love doll in the other, Dean stood on top of five chairs that were on top of the table that all the plebes held in the air over their heads. Dean, skipping the double-dog dare, went right for the throat. Everyone marveled at his lack of fear and ability to always creatively take things to the next level. Luckily for Dean, the officer in charge that night happened to be in another wing of the mess hall. As the song progressed and Dean and others exacerbated the situation, I couldn't help but think about how much punishment was coming our way.

As if the night couldn't get any rowdier, the entire plebe class started handing out cigars to all three thousand upperclassmen. Although most cadets were very health conscious, it didn't stop anyone that night. As thousands began funneling out of the two large doors at the entrance to Washington Hall, everyone began smoking their stogies in celebration of the semester's end. Although there were designated smoking areas, cadets ignored those rules, like everything else that night, and smoked right in front of the mess. For any bystanders who might have been driving by, they probably would have thought that Washington Hall was on fire. There was so much smoke billowing from 4,000 cadets standing in front of the mess hall that one wouldn't even need a cigar to be smoking that night. Most of us knew that this was the icing on the cake. There was no way the officers in charge where going to let us get away with our behavior that night.

The next morning, I was expecting to hear that Christmas break was cancelled. *How did we allow ourselves to get so crazy the night before?* As I walked past other cadets, I could hear rumors of punishment being whispered throughout the entire campus. Evidently, I wasn't the only one worried about what was going to happen. As time progressed, we kept hearing gossip of castigation but never saw any tangible consequences.

Upon our return from Christmas break, we surely expected punishment for our actions before leave. To our dismay, nothing was ever said or done. We couldn't believe the senior leaders let us get away with such acts of ill-discipline.

A year later, Christmas break was approaching once again. The anticipation from the three classes that experienced Christmas dinner last year was running high. This year, explicit orders were sent out by e-mail: Cadets will not lift tables. They will conduct themselves in a military manner throughout the entire meal. The conduct of last year's dinner will not be repeated. Additionally, there were stern instructions stating that if cigars were going to be smoked at the conclusion of dinner, it must be done in designated smoking areas. By the chatter that was running rampant throughout the Academy, it seemed like most guys weren't planning to obey the e-mail. Some say history repeats itself, but I guess only time would tell. The mind-set of the senior cadets was childlike at best. What could possibly happen to us this year? No one got in trouble last time. This was the arrogant mind-set that plagued the minds of the future leaders as they attended the Christmas dinner of 2002.

The only problem, this year the officers in charge of the school were prepared for the predictable actions of the cadets. As copycats of Chris Dean attempted to climb on top of tables, multiple officers on duty that night started pulling cadets off tables and taking names. Despite the cadets ignoring the direct orders and smoking in front of the mess hall, the multiple officers on duty simply took notes of the entire event.

That next morning we woke up worried about the potential consequences for good reason. That morning as all the Firsties woke up for breakfast formation, they read an e-mail requiring their attendance at Robinson Auditorium. Evidently, we needed to have a little chat with the Brigade Commander in charge of all cadets. We knew the jig was up. We had disobeyed a direct order and now it was time to pay the consequences.

That afternoon, the meeting was exactly what we had expected. Our mutinous activities were subjected to extreme reprimand. Luckily, there were so many people involved in the ill-behavior that no criminal charges were considered. Instead, the entire first class was on lock-down for thirty days. I think the plebes had more privileges than the soon-to-be graduating Firsties. The experience was humiliating, disgraceful, and all as a result of our own poor judgment and imprudent behavior. The punishment definitely fit the crime, and I'm sure most of the senior leaders would argue that we deserved even more.

* * *

The BLUF of this story is twofold. First, when negligent actions are not corrected immediately by leaders, it invokes complacency among followers. Second, understanding the commander's intent is the difference between leaders and followers.

It always amazes me how parents will correct their children the instant they make mistakes, but when it comes to the workplace, leaders avoid confrontation at all costs. Oftentimes, amateur leaders attempt to take on a role in which they desire their subordinate's friendship. As a result, they avoid confrontation at all costs in an attempt to maintain this status. They strive to be the nice boss or "the boss they never had." As a leader, your responsibilities are to care for your subordinates and accomplish missions. Nowhere in the previous statement did I mention that a leader needs to be their subordinates' friend. The truth is, subordinates desire a leader who takes charge. They want a person who sets the example and wouldn't ask them to complete any task they wouldn't do themselves. Experienced leaders will always lead by example.

In the story, the cadets undoubtedly deserved punishment for their actions during the first Christmas dinner. Unfortunately, nothing was said to correct any wrongdoing after the first offense. Immediately, the human psyche associates that behavior as an acceptable course of action. This poor decision to not correct the issue the following day undoubtedly added fuel to the fire during the following year when the cadets had the mind-set that no consequences would result from their actions.

In the story, you will recall that I said an e-mail was sent out to the cadets describing the expectations of how the dinner should be conducted. Leadership through e-mail is a disastrous technique.

I'm sure everyone has received an e-mail from a co-worker that is sitting five steps away. Instead of walking one office down the hall or picking up a phone to convey a message, the "e-mail weasel" will send a message about a meeting that is about to take place in five minutes. Forty-five minutes later, as you show up late to the meeting, the e-mail weasel then has the nerve to tell the boss that he sent you an e-mail. If I were the boss hearing such a comment, my immediate reply would be, "Why didn't you call?"

The problem with e-mail isn't its capability to convey a message, but rather its ability to convey the intent. When individuals refuse to handle correspondence through "the old-fashioned way," the commander's intent is always lost. In the Christmas story, if the senior leadership had held a meeting addressing their intentions, it would have drastically changed the outcome of the meal. When face-to-face leadership occurs, a different obligation to the subordinate is conveyed. Leaders intimately convey a message or need to their people, which in turn always produces a better product.

Here's a story about a leader who exemplifies the phrase "leadership through example." With little to no commander's intent, he flawlessly executed a mission that many can only dream of accomplishing with such honor.

"Like many Soldiers honored as heroes, 1st Lieutenant Christopher Dean of V Corps' 1st Armored Division and a member of the U.S. Military Academy Class of 2002, says he was just doing his job the day he earned a Silver Star for leading the rescue of a patrol ambushed in Baghdad. Dean, a platoon leader in the division's Company C, 2nd Battalion 37th Armor, based in Friedberg, Germany, was helping to hand authority for the division's mission over the incoming 1st Cavalry Division. A patrol from 1st Cavalry was ambushed in Sadr City, Baghdad. Dean rolled out immediately with four tanks under his charge. Traveling at top speed, they headed to the grid coordinates given by the besieged patrol. As soon as they arrived, the quick reaction force that Dean was leading was hit by a barrage of gunfire. 'We had rounds coming in from everywhere,' said Dean. 'It sounded like Rice Krispies popping.' One of his Soldiers was killed. Dean then led a seven-tank attack back into the engagement area to find the ambushed patrol. Their .50 caliber machine gun was taken out by enemy fire, leaving him atop the vehicle with only his M4 rifle. He was hit by shrapnel from a rocket-propelled grenade blast while leading the fight outside of his armored tank. Not letting the injury slow down his charge, Dean and his men continued forward until reaching the ambushed patrol. Now at the site, Dean and his men dismounted again to help get the patrol out of harm's way. Under heavy enemy fire they pulled out the dead and wounded and put them inside the tanks, then used one of Dean's tanks to push two damaged vehicles out of the area. Dean's team rescued nineteen Soldiers from the ambush. In a huge ceremony on October 17th, 1st Armored Division welcomed its "Iron Soldiers" home from their fifteen months in Iraq, and Dean stood before thousands of his fellow troops as a Silver Star was pinned to his uniform, to wear along with the Purple Heart he had been presented earlier."

(Joseph, 2004)

Some say history repeats itself, but I'd rather say, "No one beats the Dean."

Chris Dean
(Photo taken his senior year)

Chris Dean only minutes after receiving his Red Rider BB Gun

Chris Dean
An American War Hero like his father
(Wearing a Silver Star, three Bronze Stars, a Purple heart, two Army Commendation medals, a Combat Action Badge, and numerous others.)

8

The Shoe

It was the summer before my senior year and the conclusion of my chaotic West Point journey was in sight. I proudly donned the Firstie rank on my uniform. As a Firstie, I was king. Although there was a rank structure among the first class, it was obeyed loosely among each other. My classmates knew we would all be commissioned as second lieutenants, and therefore, be heading to the bottom of the totem pole once again. This was our time to enjoy our reign at the top as the decision makers of the school.

My first duty as a senior was to be a platoon leader during Beast Barracks. When new students show up to the Academy straight from high school, select upperclassmen put them through summer training in order to prepare them for military life and their plebe academic year. During Beast, the new cadets learn how to march, salute, shoot weapons, press uniforms, shine shoes, and many other skills that the typical civilian might picture as part of military training. Essentially, it was West Point's version of boot camp. At the end of Beast, a class of approximately 1,200 new cadets would be slowly whittled down to 1,050. This transformation from a hedonistic civilian lifestyle was a very rude awakening for some of the new hopefuls and some just couldn't cut it after those few short weeks. This was expected but definitely not condoned. We had a motto that we drilled into the heads of the new cadets: cooperate and graduate. We never left a cadet behind. If we had someone who wanted to quit, it wasn't because the chain of command gave up on him. Instead, the individual gave up on himself.

Being a platoon leader was a great responsibility. I was in charge of training forty new cadets in all of the basic skills outlined by the Commandant of Cadets. Additionally, I was in charge of five juniors, or Cows. Between the five Cows and myself, we were the enforcers and trainers of the new cadets during Beast. One of the Cows, Cadet Sergeant (CDT SGT) Moon, my platoon sergeant, was second in charge of the platoon and ultimately responsible for his four other classmates. His classmates, on the other hand, had the unique opportunity to train nine to ten new cadets each. They were the first-line supervisors and ultimately made the training happen. I would call the shots and let CDT SGT Moon implement the plan of action with his team leaders.

The night before my new cadets arrived for their first day at West Point, I memorized all forty of their first and last names, their hometowns, ages, unique skills, and any other information I had at my disposal. Some had been the valedictorian of their class and others were first in their state for running track. I would always take great pride in understanding and knowing the people I led. I believe that when leaders know the capabilities of the individuals in the group, it truly benefits the team as a whole. The next morning, the beginning of Beast was officially underway. As you might remember from the first chapter, the first day of Beast is extremely overwhelming for new cadets. The goal for the upper class was to maintain accountability as the new cadets went through numerous, different checkpoints throughout the day. One of the first stations was getting them out of their civilian clothes and into uniform. Luckily for the upper class, shirts with the new cadets' last names where handed out at the first station as they in-processed.

As the new cadets began to funnel through all of the stations and back to our platoon area, they would all officially report to me. In order for the new cadets to get assigned a room in the barracks, they must first meet their platoon leader. To prepare the new cadets for meeting their platoon leaders, the Cows would swiftly go over a memorized line that they would need to repeat upon meeting me for the first time.

The Cows would say, "New Cadets, you are about to meet your platoon leader for the first time. The last thing you want to portray is a weak image lacking the basic skills of a qualified candidate. He is standing directly to your rear and is wearing a red sash. At my command, you will conduct an about face, step up to the line that is before him, and repeat the following statement: 'Sir, New Cadet Doe reporting to the cadet in red sash for the first time as ordered.' Do you understand, new cadet?"

With their eyes wide open and so much new information pouring out of their ears, the new cadets would unequivocally respond, "Yes, Sir."

As the junior class heard the resounding response from each new candidate, they then instructed, "New Cadet, conduct an about face and execute."

As the first new cadet conducted his about face and saw me standing about twenty-five feet away, he began to walk toward me with trepidation. As the new cadet got closer, I could read his last name on his shirt. I remembered New Cadet Johnson was purely an academic guru from Memphis, Tennessee. Quickly making his way to the line that was marked on the pavement one foot in front of my position, he stopped, took a deep breath, and started the memorized lines.

"Sir, C-C-C-Cadet Johnson re-reporting to the cadet in-in the red sash, Sir!?"

"New Cadet Johnson, why are you stuttering while

trying to report to me," I said sternly.

"No excuse, Sir," Johnson answered back quickly.

"Is there something in the water down in Memphis that makes you stutter like that?" I responded back even quicker with a bold face that read "don't even try me, kid."

The utter shock on his face was priceless. Johnson just looked at me. Looking stunned, he paused briefly before slowly saying, "No, Sir."

I articulated very clearly and decisively, "New Cadet Johnson, the proper format for reporting is: 'Sir, New Cadet Johnson reporting to the cadet in red sash for the first time as ordered.' I don't need to hear the remix. I will not tolerate anything other than the standard. Do you understand my instructions?"

New Cadet Johnson, still staring at me with a weird look on his face, said, "Sir, I do."

"New Cadet Johnson, I am not ordained and I'm not reciting wedding vows to you. Do you understand your four responses or do you just have a short-term memory?"

Dumbfounded and not even getting my clever joke, Johnson didn't say anything.

"New Cadet, your four responses are: Yes, Sir. No, Sir. No excuse, Sir. And Sir, I do not understand. 'Sir, I do' is not one of your four responses. Don't let me hear it again," I quickly corrected.

"Yes Sir," Johnson responded back with a look that said "this guy can't be serious."

The only problem for Johnson and all the new cadets attending Beast that summer was that we were serious. They found that out quickly, and if they didn't, they usually didn't make it past the second day. These formalities and manners of conducting oneself were the standard for an entire year. There weren't any negotiations or ways around these standards.

Beast, as an upperclassman, was an excellent chance to begin honing the leadership skills that we had been studying the three previous years. It was amazing to see Beast Barracks from the opposite perspective of what I remembered as a plebe. The sheer terror of even going to the bathroom as a new cadet was something that we knew existed, but it was hard remembering those times because so much had happened over a three-year time frame. As a new cadet, leaving the room and walking down the hall fifteen feet to use the bathroom could sometimes result in a thirty-minute trip. If an upperclassman stopped them on their way back, they could endure a volley of questions pertaining to their required knowledge. For the most part, the new cadets' rooms were their safety zone, except during inspections.

Time during Beast Barracks took on a whole new meaning for the new cadets. For example, the short amount of time between the end of physical training (PT), 6:00 a.m., and the start of breakfast formation, 6:30 a.m., didn't allow much time for new cadets to misman-age anything. They needed to shower, put their room into inspection standards, memorize knowledge, and get dressed in uniform without any gigs.

Time was stretched so thin that when new cadets would go to the showers after PT, my upper class com-rades would shout, "Start doubling up, new cadets!"

This humiliating experience meant as one guy was putting shampoo on his head, his buddy would rinse off in the water, therefore creating a vicious cycle of men get-ting showers two at a time per shower head. Not a second was wasted, and if a person was uncomfortable standing next to a naked man, this phobia ended quickly.

As the weeks went by, I had a new cadet that we re-ferred to as an all-star. At West Point, an all-star actually meant the opposite of what most might think. An all-star was a guy who would take up the majority of your time to train. Most often, it wasn't because the all-star shouldn't be at the Academy. He just had a harder time adapting from civilian to military life. Well, our all-star's name was New Cadet Lee, and to put things nicely, he had some difficulties during the first few weeks at the school. Although Lee didn't start out so hot that summer, a major event occurred that created a complete role reversal for the good.

Before every meal, we would have a formation to get accountability of all the new cadets attending Beast. The formation was a standard Army structure that most have seen in movies. All the Soldiers stand behind their leaders and as the chain of command collects the information throughout the ranks, the accountability is then passed to the higher echelons. In approximately 2 minutes, the commander of Beast Barracks would have accountability of all 1,300 students. It was very structured and very expeditious. Before this occurred, the new cadets were required to stand at parade rest in formation ten minutes prior to the command of "fall-in." This rule was a requirement because it gave the chain of command an opportunity to inspect uniforms and review knowledge that the new cadets were attempting to memorize. The Cows would generally monitor the new cadets' early arrival as the Firsties would slowly stroll down just minutes prior to fall-in. As I would walk out the doors from Eisenhower Hall to our company's formation, I would walk past each platoon. Some platoons would be doing push-ups while others were reciting knowledge in unison. For the normal person, it would look like complete chaos, but there was definitely a method to the madness.

I would walk up to my platoon and they would all greet me with the platoon greeting. "Mount up, Sir," each new cadet would shout as I made my way around the formation. Our platoon's name was Regulators and our motto was "Mount Up." I stole the theme from a Warren G rap CD. It was tacky, yet delightful, and the new cadets loved to say it. They all knew where I got it, so I think they liked having something that wasn't a standard Army name and motto. We were always the loudest platoon when we would report our numbers to higher. I would shout, "REGULATORS" and all forty new cadets would resound behind me, "MOUNT UP." *It was fun.*

On one particular morning formation, I headed down about five minutes early to see what was going on with my platoon. As I started walking through the squads, I came across New Cadet Lee. Looking at his face, I could tell he hadn't even shaved that morning.

"New Cadet Lee, did you shave this morning?" I questioned angrily.

Lee paused briefly as if he didn't understand my question, then replied, "No, Sir."

Frustrated at this point, I said, "Lee, you grow facial hair as fast as a hairless cat, but that doesn't mean that you can neglect shaving every morning."

At this point, CDT SGT Moon and Lee's team leader had heard my comment and were chomping at the bit to get a piece of Lee. As a result, I stepped back and heard CDT SGT Moon tell Lee that he needed to write down on a piece of paper "I will shave every morning, despite the lack of facial hair I grow" 500 times and have it slipped under his door before Taps that night.

CDT SGT Moon was an extremely astute individual. I was thrilled to have him as my platoon sergeant because he didn't miss anything. One of his standard punishments was making the new cadets write sentences. While some upperclassmen would submit the new cadets to physical punishments, others, like CDT SGT Moon, would specialize in mental retribution.

Lee, showing no emotion regarding his new punishment, unflinchingly said, "Yes, Sergeant."

Just as CDT SGT Moon was getting ready to walk away, he happened to look down at Lee's unpolished black leather shoes. Pausing for a second, Moon looked around as if he was going to ask Lee a secret question. As he leaned forward and put his right hand by the side of his mouth, he whispered into Lee's ear.

He said, "What did you use, a Snickers bar or a 100 Grand?"

Puzzled, and looking as if had been asked the riddle to finding a nuclear warhead, Lee responded back, "Sergeant, I do not understand."

Moon, really pausing and building some drama this time, enunciated very clearly and shouted, "Lee, I'm asking you what kind of candy bar you used to shine your shoes this morning."

As Lee started to respond, he was quickly interrupted by CDT SGT Moon as he went on a rampage. SGT Moon moved rapidly to the front of the formation and began shouting.

"Lee, post to the front of formation." Moon was moving like his hair was on fire.

"All right, everyone in this platoon is going to do push-ups for not helping New Cadet Lee shine his shoes and shave this morning."

All the new cadets in the platoon shouted back, "Yes, Sergeant."

Upon Lee's arrival at the front of the platoon, CDT SGT Moon said, "Lee, you are going to count the push-ups and stand right here while they all push for you."

Needless to say, the look on Lee's face showed everyone that he felt remorse for his actions. Meanwhile, I just stood on the side of the formation and watched my outstanding Cows work their magic. CDT SGT Moon understood the human psyche and played that to his advantage on numerous occasions.

Although CDT SGT Moon was using different techniques to try and motivate Lee, nothing really worked. He continued to have issues with his shoes and definitely didn't understand the gist of what was required. His effort output was at 100 percent, but he just wasn't firing on all pistons like the other new cadets. That night, I went to CDT SGT Moon's room to discuss the next week's schedule of training. As I pushed open his door, I looked down and saw at least thirty pieces of paper all folded up like love notes on the floor.

I looked at Moon and said, "Wow, these little buggers love you! How long does it take you to write them back each night?"

Moon just laughed as I entered the room. As I started toward his desk, I kicked all the pieces of paper, full of sentences that the new cadets had written, off to the side. As I glanced down, I saw a bundle of at least ten pages that said, "I will not call Cadet Sergeant Moon, Ma'am. He is a male cadet non-commissioned officer." One would be amazed at what some of these new cadets would say in the stress of answering questions. As I pulled up a chair and started going over all the requirements that we needed to teach for the next week, Moon looked at me with frustration.

He said, "What the hell are we going to do about Lee?" I thought for a second but really didn't have an answer.

I looked at Moon and said, "Listen, 10 percent of the people who work for you will take 90 percent of your time. We just need to give him a little more time and find out what motivates him."

"I know," Moon replied. That night when I went back to my room, I started thinking about how we could get New Cadet Lee back on track. The one thing that Lee wasn't doing was learning from his mistakes. He was motivated and I definitely didn't think he was performing poorly on purpose. I was convinced that there was something the chain of command could do to turn this guy around.

The next morning, I woke up exhausted. Amazingly,

I was getting less sleep as a platoon leader than when I was a new cadet going through Beast. It was unexpected but well worth the enjoyment of leading Soldiers. That morning, as I walked down to breakfast formation, I could hear the rumblings from the second class. I knew something was wrong.

As I walked out the door and looked at my platoon, I saw every upperclassman huddled around the spot where Lee stood in formation. This wasn't going to be good. As I got closer, I saw CDT SGT Moon's face directly in front of Lee's and he was really upset. Moon looked like he was going to burst a blood vessel on the side of his neck as he questioned the frightened New Cadet Lee. CDT SGT Moon, upon seeing that I was on my way out the door, began to shout in my direction.

"Sir... Sir... You've got to see this!" CDT SGT Moon shouted as he directed me toward Lee with his arms like a ground traffic controller. As I got closer to the huddle of upperclassmen surrounding Lee, I heard CDT SGT Moon continue speaking.

"Do you think this is a game? Do you really think that you can make a mockery of this institution?" As I stood next to my platoon sergeant, who appeared to be out of breath, he looked dumbfounded at what he was dealing with. CDT SGT Moon said, "Sir, look at Lee's shoes. He thought it might be funny to mock everyone in the chain of command by shining only his right shoe."

As I looked down at Lee's shoes to see what my stellar junior was talking about, I saw my reflection in just one of his shoes. The right shoe looked like Lee had shined the shoe for at least ten hours, as its pure-glass finish looked even better than CDT SGT Moon's shoes. The only problem was that his left shoe looked like he had just finished playing a soccer game in it. SGT Moon continued his verbal lashings at Lee.

"You obviously know how to shine a shoe because

this one on the right looks better than anything I've seen all summer. It's your arrogance of parading your ability to do so in spite of the rules that I can't understand. You did this on purpose. You're mocking us!" he screamed.

You could tell by Moon's sincerity that he meant the words he was saying. The upper class truly believed Lee was making a mockery of them by only shining one of his shoes. As I listened to all of the attacks against Lee, I softly yet assertively told everyone to stop and give me a couple of seconds with the delinquent subordinate.

I called New Cadet Lee out of formation and took him off to the side where his classmates couldn't hear what I was saying.

As he stood at attention, I leaned forward and whispered into his ear so no one else could hear, "Learn from your mistakes and you will prosper, but if you reveal disgust to those who highlight your blunders, you will certainly fail."

That was it; nothing more, nothing less. There was a lapse of silence before I walked away. SGT Moon was anxious to get Lee back into formation, so he quickly called for his return. At that point, it was like someone had turned off the volume in Lee's ears. All the shouting from the upperclassmen wasn't even heard. Lee knew what had happened. For the rest of the day, you could tell that there was something eating away at him like a snake slowly devouring its prey. It was a long day for New Cadet Lee as the upper class relentlessly directed any and all of their frustrations toward him.

The next morning was the dawn of a new day. Lee was a new cadet, literally. When he showed up for the morning formation, his uniform was immaculate and both his shoes were flawless. His attitude was as positive as a Firstie on graduation. One could tell there was something different from the start of that day. The great thing about this story is that Lee continued to prosper for the rest of the summer. By the end of Beast, he was one of the strongest contributors to the platoon. It was a transformation that no one had expected.

One might be curious as to what I meant two paragraphs above when I said, "Lee knew what had happened." What I'm referring to is that Lee realized that *I had taken his shoe during the night and shined it to perfection.* I was the one responsible for putting him in such a terrible situation that day. He knew that I was correcting him in such a way that would force him to listen, learn, and succeed or be negligent, dogmatic, and fail.

I don't mean to brag, but I can shine shoes really well. All that practice during the three previous years evidently got the best of me. I had a technique that I called the fire-freeze that I would use to shine shoes to perfection in very little time. To get a "spit-shine" finish on a leather shoe, which will actually show your reflection if done correctly, usually requires a lot of work. To start seeing your reflection, it will take a couple of weeks of putting hundreds of coats of polish on a shoe just to get even close. I could take a pair of leather shoes and by using the fire-freeze technique, I could turn dull leather-bound shoes into what appeared to be glass- covered masterpieces over night.

The night that CDT SGT Moon and I had the conversation pertaining to motivating New Cadet Lee, I got the idea of how to fix his behavior. I knew I needed to do something drastic to get his attention. Then once I got his attention, I needed to lead him down the path of self-motivated progress. That night was a hot night. Lee's door, like all the other new cadets' doors, was left open to compensate for the heat that saturated the stone buildings each night. Around 1:30 a.m., I walked past his room and happened to take one of his shoes. I took that shoe back to my room and proceeded to conduct the fire-freeze technique for the next hour. I first lit the shoe polish on fire and spread thick heavy coats all over the barren shoe. As the polish would dry, I continued to apply more thick heavy coats. After about fifteen minutes, the shoe was inundated with more polish than Lee had in his entire room. Now for step two. In order to get the polish to really solidify, I then wrapped the shoe in a plastic bag and threw it in the company freezer for an additional fifteen minutes. Once I pulled the shoe out of the freezer it was nice and cold and looked like somebody had applied well over 1,000 coats of polish. At this point the technique was simple: simply apply little amounts of polish and water in order to give the shoe its mirror finish. It was now 2:30 a.m. and I needed to get to bed, so I quietly returned Lee's one shoe back to his room and waited until the next morning.

* * *

The BLUF of this story is that strong leaders learn from criticism and don't become combative when approached with perceived denigration.

I once read an article by a professional journalist that was titled "Deal with Criticism like a Pro." It instantly turned my stomach. What a terrible title for a motivational paper. Most can deal with criticism with little or no effort. It's learning from criticism that's extremely hard. In the previous story, I learned a valuable lesson from one of my subordinates. Yes, learning can come from subordinates, peers, and superiors. Lee was a living, breathing example of how to take constructive criticism and learn from his mistakes. More importantly, he did it without developing a negative attitude toward me or anyone else in the chain of command. That second part is the piece that people intrinsically have a difficult time controlling.

Everyone has seen the coworker who gets bitter instantly when anyone critiques or reprimands his work. This is a person who has reached a dead end in life. A wise man once said, "Show me a person who knows everything and I'll show you a failure." Most people are quick to place their failures or shortfalls with their neighbors but reap the same neighbor's successes as their own. Everyday across America you see parents blaming teachers for their children's poor academic performance. This is something that my mind can't comprehend. I know when I was a young kid and I brought my report card home to my parents, if I presented poor grades, it was my fault and not my teacher's. This "blame it on someone else" mind-set is a ghastly habit, and one must always remember to watch his own habits. Habits become character, and over time, one's character becomes his destiny.

Leaders welcome criticism; they seek it. At West Point, we would conduct after action reviews (AARs) specifically to review our shortfalls.

At the end of an exercise, the leader would say, "Give me three positives and three negatives that we can sustain or fix for the next similar training event."

At times, I've seen the AAR turn into a back-patting party where everyone is solely talking about their successes. I've always seen the strong leaders take charge of this situation and stop the group abruptly.

"All right, enough with the success stories. I know you're awesome, and you clearly know you're awesome, but how are we going to improve? Smith, stand up and give me some improves," the leader would remark.

There's always room for improvement, and when a leader fails to identify failures, future missions or endeavors will never improve. A great quote from General Colin Powell states, "There is no secret to success. It is the result of preparation, hard work, and learning from failure."

9

The Navy Loves Water

The year was 1904 and it was early in the morning. As the enlisted detail arrived at Trophy Point to fire the reveille cannon, they realized something was amiss. Every morning at West Point, a large cannon is fired and followed by a bugler's call of reveille. The cannon is so massive that the boom can be heard miles away. Looking around in utter amazement, the members of the detail realized someone had removed the cannon from its usual resting place. Out of options, the bugler began playing without an official boom to start the day. After reporting the information through the chain of command, a large search for the enormous cannon was underway. Everyone knew it couldn't have gone far, considering the mere size and weight of the lost cannon. Many suspected that it had been pushed over the steep cliff that surrounded the scenic Trophy Point, but after an intense search, nothing was found. Rumors among the Corps of Cadets spread rampant in reference to the cannon's location. As the day progressed, one observant individual happened to notice the muzzle of a massive weapon peeking over the parapet of the clock tower on the academic building. Soon, cadets and instructors were scrambling to the top of the clock tower to see if the cannon had been located. To everyone's surprise, they found the massive missing mortar piece. Flabbergasted at how such an event could occur, the Generals in charge of the school launched an investigation into how the cannon could possibly have been moved to the top of the building in only one night. Even more importantly, how did the perpetrators of this endeavor manage to move the weapon unnoticed by the two roving guards patrolling the area? After two weeks, the investigation was found to be inconclusive and the cannon was removed from the clock tower by the Army Corps of Engineers with the use of a crane. A careful inspection found no indication that a pulley apparatus had been used; there were no marks on the floor and no marks on the walls leading to the fifth story of the building where the cannon sat. Conjecture and rumor throughout history has suggested that a young cadet named Douglas MacArthur was responsible for the mission.

Ninety-nine years later, I sat in the same building where the notorious cannon incident took place. I was listening to some of my friends talk about their plans for a spirit mission of their own. The old academic building was retrofitted into dorms and was now called Pershing Barracks. This is where I lived for three out of my four years at the Academy. In fact, my friends Todd Cody and Nick Ryan lived in the room directly beneath the clock tower on the fourth floor. For over a hundred years, "spirit missions" have been conducted at the Academy as a means of boosting morale among the Corps of Cadets.

For an outsider, impractical missions like this might seem to have no point or value. To the cadets, on the other hand, these missions serve as a nostalgic tradition that creates competition and satire throughout the school. Most spirit missions are conducted during important weeks. For example, many spirit missions are conducted during the weeks of the Army-Air Force football game and the Army-Navy football game. Despite the prevalence of spirit missions during those two weeks, it was still common to hear of spirit missions being conducted throughout other times of the year. The rules for spirit missions were simple: don't get caught, don't talk about the mission, and don't do something that has already been done.

This was an exceptional time of year for spirit missions because it was the start of Army-Navy week. For the entire week leading up to the Saturday game, numerous events would occur to increase spirit throughout the Corps. For example, each school has a competition to see who can do the most push-ups throughout the week leading up to the game. The push-ups were counted through the honor system, and at the end of each day, everyone would report their totals through the chain of command. In an effort to produce higher numbers, companies would tape off square boxes all over the floor that were turned into push-up boxes. If anyone stepped inside any of the boxes, they would have to do the number of push-ups that was written inside the box. It was standard protocol to put a massive, unavoidable box around the entrance to all the plebes' rooms. Typically, every plebe would do well over 200 push-ups per day during Army-Navy week. At the game, they would announce the winner of the competition, but Navy usually had such low numbers that it wasn't even a competition.

As my friends and I continued sharing stories and ideas for potential missions, we determined that we needed something that was a lot more spirited than doing push-ups. A few of my friends had a professor who was a naval officer, and as a result, they kept plugging for a mission against him. Hearing the idea sparked a memory from when I was a plebe during Army-Navy week. I began telling the story to my friends who were very anxious for ideas.

I told them that during the Army-Navy week when I was a plebe, we had an exchange midshipman from Annapolis assigned to our company. Every year, there is an agreement between the Naval Academy and the Air Force

Academy in which a few students can attend school as an exchange cadet for one semester. The only time this exchange is available is during the first semester of a cadet's Cow year. Typically, many cadets apply for the few five to eight slots that are offered by each of the two schools. As one might expect, getting chosen for this option was highly selective and only the best from each school got the opportunity to be in the program. An even exchange was conducted in order to keep continuity of numbers between schools. After the semester is over, all the exchange cadets and midshipmen return to their alma mater and continue on their way. It is considered common courtesy for the plebes to treat the exchange upperclassmen with the same respect as their West Point upperclassmen. This was an unwritten rule among schools because we knew they had endured the same antics during their plebe year.

The particular midshipman who was assigned to our company treated the plebes with respect and really didn't harass us very much compared to the West Point upperclassmen. The one thing we found amusing about him was how self-conscious he was with respect to his image. This guy habitually wore cologne and would always be in front of the mirror after showers. This was uncommon for anyone at the Academy. If a guy would act this way, it was usually because he was getting ready to go on a date or was trying to impress someone. Instead, he had a habit of conducting himself in this manner every day. Most probably would have described him as a "pretty boy." As a plebe, there was obviously nothing I could say, but I would often hear the upperclassmen making fun of him for being so concerned with his hygiene. One day, as I was finishing up in the shower, one of the upperclassmen came into the bathroom to use the urinal. The midshipman, as usual, was positioned right in front of the mirror grooming himself when he saw the upperclassman walk into the bathroom. In a hurry, the upperclassman conducted his business at the urinal and began to exit the room. Offended that the upperclassman wasn't going to wash his hands, the midshipman politely remarked, "You know, at Annapolis they teach us to wash our hands when we are finished going to the bathroom." Laughing and obviously annoyed by the midshipman's comment, the West Point upperclassman quickly replied, "Hey, Squid. They teach us not to piss on our hands here." Disgruntled, the midshipman continued trimming his nose hairs.

The midshipman wasn't a hard upperclassman to deal with, so the plebes actually didn't mind him being in the company — that was until Army-Navy week. In an effort to cause as many problems as possible, the Squid, as they were commonly named, was trying to disrupt any and all spirit programs that were being conducted that week. At night, when everyone was sleeping, he would go into the halls and tear down posters and rip all the tape off the floor that was being used for push-ups. In fact, he started hazing the plebes really bad. At meals, he would make table duties very difficult so we couldn't even eat. All of my classmates had endured enough of this guy's wrath. We thought he was even starting to anger the upperclassmen for picking on us so much. In the middle of the week as we were just getting ready to finish our laundry duties, we heard a knock at the door. As we called the room to attention, one of the plebes shouted for the upperclassmen to enter the room. When the door was flung open, one of the Firsties was standing at the entrance to the room. Anytime an upperclassman is in a room with a plebe, the door needs to remain open, but this time he closed the door. Feeling a little awkward, we couldn't imagine what was going to be said. The Firstie began speaking. "Why are you guys letting that Squid push you around like that?" Everyone in the room just looked around and really didn't have a response to his question. We were always told to treat him just like any other upper-class cadet. The Firstie continued, "Well, between you and me, I'm giving you full authority to put him in his place. You guys look pathetic out there." Before we could even ask what he meant by "put him in his place," the Firstie stormed out of the room with a look of disappointment on his face. Needless to say, we were ecstatic to be "given permission" to seek revenge on the manicured midshipman who was making our lives a living hell that week. Since the Firstie didn't give us any specific guidelines, we interpreted his remarks as not having any limitations.

Anxious to take our vengeance, we started plotting and planning the best course of action to take against the Squid. We knew the plan needed to be extremely detailed and the operation needed to be executed flawlessly. The first order of business was trying to figure out the most fatal blow that could be delivered. Quickly, we came to an agreement that our plan needed to involve his infatuation with the mirror. It was obvious that this was his weak spot. As we developed our detailed plan, many of the plebes became giddy with excitement.

After spending a day of planning and preparing, it was time to execute our mission. That night after the Squid had finished his shower, we decided to get him when he least expected our assault. Just as he entered his room after an hour-long escapade in the bathroom, twenty plebes stormed his room. We had a couple of football and rugby players up front while the rest of the plebes were ready for phase two in the bathroom. As the football and rugby players stormed his room, he knew the jig was up. In a frantic rush, the Squid tried to run out the door like a criminal trying to escape from a sting operation. At this point, survival of the fittest took effect. Notwithstanding any formalities, the Squid came out throwing punches in an effort to scare the massive plebes who were ready to take him into custody. The punches were like a child playing patty-cake with the brawny Shannon Worthen, who was sporting thirty-six stitches in his forehead from a rugby game during the previous week. Needless to say, they brought the Squid to the ground and duct taped his hands and feet together quicker than a cowboy roping a calf at a rodeo. Despite being hog-tied and lying on the ground, the Squid was still kicking and screaming for help. At this point, everyone in the building could hear what was going on and instead of helping their fellow upperclassman, they stood outside the door with digital cameras, taking pictures. As the Squid started chanting "Go Navy, beat Army," the plebes quickly pulled off another piece of tape and placed it over his mouth. The tape quickly put an end to that nonsense shouting. At this point, you could tell that the Squid thought the game was over, but to his surprise, it was just getting started. Instead, this was when his worst nightmare was about to come true. The buff plebes looked down at the Squid as he lay helpless on the floor and said, "All right, Squid. We're now going to take you to your favorite place." By the look in his eyes, one could tell he had no idea where he was going. Two of the plebes reached down and grabbed the Squid by his duct-taped arms and began pulling him down the hall like a dead animal. Amazingly, his wavy blond hair was still intact as he was dragged a hundred feet toward the bathroom. Numerous upperclassmen had gathered in the hall and weren't saying a thing about the incident that was unfolding. As the Squid was dragged within a couple feet of the bathroom, he could hear the horror that awaited him. As the buzz of the hair clippers initiated, everyone in the hall could see his legs start kicking like an animal that was ready to be slaughtered.

After we were done in the bathroom, it was hard to tell which was smoother: his legs, armpits, or head. The hair was collected and placed in a plastic bag and hung in the company area. Above the displayed bag read a sign "Go Army, Beat Navy." The most enjoyable part of the whole episode was watching him reunite with his friends from Annapolis at the football game on Saturday. The looks on their faces were priceless as they knew he had endured a wonderful Army-Navy week at West Point. It was a bitter 22-degree game and I'm sure he enjoyed every second.

After hearing this hilarious story, my friends all agreed that something that hostile couldn't be conducted to their Navy instructor. Instead, they felt that their identities needed to be withheld. They still needed to get a passing grade in the class and the last thing they wanted was to spend a summer at STAP. However, they did complain that their Navy instructor was conducting himself in a similar manner to the Squid. They said he was making their lives a living hell that week.

"If that guy gives us another test or quiz this week, I think I'm going to lose my mind," my one friend confessed.

As we discussed numerous different courses of action, they really couldn't decide on anything that was worthwhile. Frustrated, they left my room and promised to let me know if they decided on anything.

The next day, I passed one of the guys as he was discussing the potential spirit mission against his naval professor. He informed me that they had managed to acquire the key to their teacher's office through a faculty source. He wouldn't give me the specifics of the mission, but he assured me that I wouldn't be disappointed. At this point, I was very curious to know what those guys had up their sleeves. By the look on his face, I could tell it was going to be splendid.

The following morning, I woke up and began reading the e-mails I had received during the night. One was titled "FW: FW: FW: FW: The Navy Loves Water." Of course, I opened it first. When I opened the document,

I could see that there were two pictures attached to the e-mail. Suspecting that the e-mail originated with one of my friends, I scrolled through the long distribution lists to see where the document had started. At the end of all the forwarded messages, I saw the e-mail had been sent from a civilian hotmail account. By the address, there was no way of telling who the owner of the e-mail address was. I anticipated that the pictures had to be juicy. As I opened the first picture, it showed three guys standing in front of a door. By the looks of the name tape on the door, it was the office of the Navy instructor my friends had mentioned two days prior. My suspicions were confirmed at this point. I knew these were my friends and I was in high hopes that they wouldn't let me down with a lame spirit mission. As I looked at the picture, I thought it was odd that all three of them were wearing ski masks and shirts that said "Go Army, Beat Navy." Even more peculiar, they were each drinking water out of Dixie cups. I closed the picture and shrugged my shoulders, trying to understand the point of the image. Then as I clicked on the next icon, everything became quite clear. To my surprise, the next image showed the naval instructor's office filled with Dixie cups full of water. Every horizontal surface in the room was covered: chairs, shelves, desks, filing cabinets, and even the coffee maker was blanketed. The thousands of filled cups stacked side by side resembled the numerous lights of a gigantic electric billboard that could be found in Times Square. There wasn't an inch of space left in the entire office that didn't have those little cups sitting on it. I could see in the picture that they had left a little room for the door to swing open. This way, in the morning when the Navy instructor came to work and opened his door, he would be inundated with the massive cleanup that awaited him.

Later that day I passed one of my friends who had conducted this incredible mission. With a big grin on his face, he said nothing more than, "Beat Navy." I gave him a head nod and replied back, "Drown them in the water."

* * *

The BLUF of this story is twofold. First, every ounce of a leader is filled with a competitive spirit. Second, leaders take pride in producing detailed plans on how to defeat their enemy/competitor.

I remember playing baseball as a young kid. It was my passion and lifeblood. Even as a young child, it would make my ears ring when I would hear a coach say, "Just as long as everyone had fun, that's all that matters." In the back of my mind I wanted to scream. There was nothing that I hated more than losing. Once I began attending the Military Academy, I found myself surrounded by individuals who shared this same mind-set. The only fun thing for a leader is winning. Some might view this stance as cruel or cold blooded, but the fact of the matter is clear: individuals who aren't thwarted by failure are followers.

I've mentioned numerous times throughout this book how everything at West Point would turn into a competition. Whether the contest was lifting tables in the air during Christmas dinner or having the highest grades in an Engineering class, the Corps of Cadets breeds leaders who must compete and win. Some individuals have an ill-conceived notion of this and they compete at overly intense levels. They believe this type of leader provokes a "zero-defect" environment. Amateur leaders may place this kind of undue stress upon their subordinates, but proven leaders adopt a different style of competitiveness. They understand that every battle can't be won, but that every war will be. They believe that in competition, a loser only exists when the opponent admits that he has been beaten. As a result, the experienced leaders take the lessons learned from whitewash and respect their competitors for their ability to take advantage of their lapse of judgment. This doesn't mean the antagonism is over; most leaders might argue it has just begun. Strong leaders will always accept their shortfalls and respect their defeat in order to build on the lessons learned and propagate champions from the knowledge gained. In the end, the real competitor and his subordinates will always be victorious. This competitive nature is so important to the fundamental steps of being a leader at West Point that one of the first pieces of knowledge a plebe must memorize deals with this very subject. Within the first week, the upperclassmen ensure that the new cadets memorize a message from Douglas MacArthur, which states, "From the Far East I send you one single thought, one sole idea – written in red on every beachhead from Australia to Tokyo – There is no substitute for Victory!"

Detailed planning is the backbone that enables experienced leaders to be victorious in competition. Are you the type of person who doesn't write anything down on a calendar? You might be surprised how important this simple action is to any leader's ability to conduct successful operations. This is the most simple and basic tool used by leaders to systematically plan and implement tasks to their subordinate organizations. To the outlying individuals, maintaining and updating a calendar is an annoying duty required by their superiors. However, to the managers, the calendar is a template that describes how goals are going to be accomplished.

Taking a closer look at the specific tasks on a calendar, one might realize that simply stating ambiguous guidance is futile to its existence. Anytime a leader issues a task during detailed planning, the subordinate needs to know the five W's associated with the task: Who is going to attend or execute the assignment, What is the mission statement or intent of the job, When is the deadline associated with the mission, Where will the job take place, and Why is the mission important to be victorious? Before I continue, I want to point out a pet peeve I have regarding young leaders who use the phrase "As soon as possible" (ASAP). I hate it! Leaders need to avoid using this phrase at all costs. The meaning of ASAP to one individual might mean a completely different thing to the leader in charge. Anytime an experienced leader tasks a subordinate to complete a mission, he needs to give a specified time associated with the deadline. Consider the following two scenarios:

Scenario 1: "Cadet Johnson, you are required to memorize MacArthur's message by 1400 hours tomorrow. Please let me know at least 5 hours prior to the suspense if you are not going to be able to complete the specified task." The next day, Johnson completes the task on time.

Scenario 2: "Cadet Johnson, you need to memorize MacArthur's message ASAP." The next day, Johnson explains that he had a doctor's appointment and 7 hours of homework and didn't have time to start the memorization.

In this story, the spirit missions serve as a droll example of how detailed planning is used to be victorious in competition. Looking back at the reveille cannon story from 1904, one must marvel at the planning and execution that the young cadets would have conducted in order to achieve such a competitive and spirited feat. Although a lot of controversy has surrounded that event, very few know that an interview took place years later between Major (MAJ) George Pappas and Five-Star General Douglas MacArthur. MAJ Pappas was a West Point graduate from the class of 1944 and was tasked with finding a speaker for the Founders' Day dinner, an annual event at the Academy. MAJ Pappas contacted the retired General in New York City and met with him in order to discuss the specifics of his speech that would be given the following week. During the meeting, MAJ Pappas asked the brave question regarding the mysterious event that took place when MacArthur was a cadet. Below is an excerpt from Pappas' manuscripts pertaining to the meeting in January of 1953.

"MacArthur said, "Major, I've done most of the talking. Don't you have any questions?" I swallowed a couple of times and then blurted out, "Yes, Sir, were you the one who put the Reveille gun on the clock tower when you were a cadet?" MacArthur began to laugh. "No," he said. "I did not, I wish I had, and I am flattered to think that I have been given credit for that prank." I asked if he knew who had done it. He replied that his classmate, Hugh Johnson, had led the group involved. I asked if he had known the gun was going to be moved. "No," he replied. "I did not. I was the First Captain and would have had to report it if I knew about it. However, I do know how it was done. Johnson described the activity to me many years later." MacArthur then related in detail how Hugh Johnson and his small group of assistants planned, practiced, and accomplished their mission. "During that era, two enlisted sentries patrolled the cadet area: one walked from the Academic Building (today's Pershing Barracks) to the Gymnasium on the site of today's Washington Hall. Here, he met another sentry, who marched along the row of officers' quarters on the western edge of the Plain. The two would meet at the Gymnasium, stop and speak briefly, and then reverse their patrol. Johnson timed the sentry's walk from the Academic Building to the Gymnasium and the brief stop before the return trip. This consistently took between 14 and 17 minutes. The next step was to determine the time required to disassemble the gun and move each part across the plain to a spot near the entryway between the Academic Building and the Barracks. The wheels were removed and simply rolled across the plain. Then the tube was removed from the carriage, and the carriage placed on two blankets for transport to a spot near the Barracks. The most difficult task was moving the heaviest piece, the tube, which also was placed on blankets and carried by four cadets. For the dry run, the only parts actually carried into the area were the wheels. On the night selected – a dark, moonless sky brightened only slightly by the gas lights in front of the Barracks – the cadets dashed across the plain and disassembled the gun. The wheels then were rolled across the grass and laid flat. The next time the sentry passed, the wheels were carried across the street, into the area, and leaned against the wall of the Academic Building. Next, the carriage was carried across the grass and into the area. The heavy tube was the last piece moved. The group stopped at least three times, lowering their burden to the ground and taking a few minutes of much needed rest. Finally, the tube was in the area."

What was next? Did Johnson and his fellow conspirators rig a pulley system to raise the gun part to the top of the Clock Tower? When I asked GEN MacArthur if this was what was done, he laughed heartily and explained exactly how the gun was raised to the tower. Each piece of the burden was taken into the Academic

Building, placed in the elevator, and taken to the top floor. From there, three steps led to a door to the roof, which was only about six feet below the top of the tower. In the meantime, several cadets climbed to the top of the Clock Tower via the spiral stairway inside. Each piece of the gun then was wrapped in blankets to prevent any damage to the masonry of the tower walls. There was no problem lifting the wheels; two cadets held each wheel as high as possible while the tower crew pulled on ropes fastened to the wheel. The carriage took a bit longer, but it too was soon on the roof of the tower. Both groups sat back for a short rest while other cadets on the tower roof attached the wheels to the carriage. Then the tube was slowly and carefully raised, a few inches at a time. At last, it was lifted over the parapet and placed on the carriage."

(Pappas, 2008)

Interesting Fact: Hugh Samuel Johnson was the first graduate of West Point from the State of Oklahoma. He became a General Officer and was also the first administrator of the NRA after being appointed by President Roosevelt.

(Reichenberger, 2010)

10

Having your Cake and Eating it Too

Staring at random objects, mesmerized in deep thought, were common occurrences for me at the Academy. Looking back at the experience, I attribute the behavior to dealing with so many quandaries all at the same time. A cadet would often be sorting through an entire day of tests, military requirements, and physical obligations that needed executed before the day's end. On one particular morning, as I experienced this zombie-like feeling, I was sitting in the mess hall getting ready to eat breakfast. It was my Firstie year and I was staring at my glass of orange juice. Despite my lack of peripheral expression, I was worrying about the three major tests I had to take later in the day. I studied two hours for each test the night before, but I should have studied four. There was never enough time to prepare for all the requirements, so managing time and academic requirements became a calculated juggling act. As I systematically calculated the risk associated with my decision from the night before, I was startled awake from my daydream. Out of the corner of my eye, I saw one of the plebes sitting at the end of the table quickly rendered a salute and make an announcement. He was talking to a small box sitting directly in front of him on the table.

"Sir, may I eat you?" the plebe said to the box.

The plebe had a very serious look on his face as he paused and lowered his salute. The incident shouldn't have startled me because it happened every morning. Just like every other morning, the plebe never heard a response from his box of Cap'n Crunch cereal. After completing the requirement to salute the captain pictured on the front of the box, the plebe started opening his cereal. I looked back at my glass of orange juice and continued in deep thought. By the looks of everyone else at the table, they were just as quiet and not in the mood for the plebes to make any mistakes with duties that morning.

For the typical civilian, mealtime is the most enjoyable part of the day. It is a chance for people to break from a stressful job and enjoy a delightful meal. Eating in America has almost become a way of life. On Friday night, most Americans consider going to eat at a fancy restaurant as an activity opposed to a source of nutrition. This type of hobby shouldn't be frowned upon, but instead, recognized as American culture. Realizing that food is a soothing contrivance for Americans, some might consider meals at the United States Military Academy to be analogous. This ill-conceived notion is far from the truth. One of the most difficult parts of a plebe's day at West Point is eating a meal. My personal experiences of eating meals as a plebe were the most dreadful part of the day. Plebes have no choice but to interact with upperclassmen during meals. As a result, it requires them to prepare and plan for every event that could potentially unfold.

Chapter seven serves as a terrible example of what it is like to eat a meal at West Point. The reality of the situation is the mess hall is a regimented area that has very strict rules and regulations that cadets must obey. The tables in the mess hall are long and slender with one chair on each end and four chairs on each of side. A Firstie with the highest rank at the table sits in the "father seat" at the end of the table. The rest of the cadets sitting at the table systematically sit according to rank order. As a result, the plebes sit at the exact opposite end of the table from the Firsties. In order to keep continuity among the Corps, an equal number of cadets from each year group are placed at each table. This way lessons and traditions are passed through the ranks during every meal.

Because of the massive size and the twenty-five-minute requirement to conduct a meal, the only way all the students can be fed is through detailed planning. Once all the cadets are assembled at their seats, waiters bring the meals on large plates to the center of each table. Each platter has enough servings for everyone at the table. Typically there is one waiter for every eight tables. The waiter is more like a courier than an individual you might find at a typical restaurant. He delivers the large package of food and then he's done. After he delivers the food, his job is complete until the meal is over and the massive cleanup operation commences. Once the food package is delivered, all the dishes are sent to the end of the table in order for the plebes to present each dish to the upper-classmen. Like anything else at the Academy, presenting the dishes to the upperclassmen has an exact format that must be followed. The general idea of all the plebe duties is that all food that's brought to the table is presented or announced to the upper class before people can start putting food on their plate.

While the plebes are waiting for the server to bring the food to the table, they present the drink that will be served for the meal. This becomes a difficult task because they need to fill all the glasses in rank order and remember each upperclassman's drink preference. This duty becomes even more frustrating when the upper class requires a specific number of ice cubes per glass. At the end of each table where the highest-ranking cadet sits, there are eleven different condiments for everyone's use. Although the types of condiments available never change, keeping accountability of all the condiments proves to be an arduous task for plebes. Typically, as one of the plebes is announcing or presenting the food, his classmate will walk to the head of the table and "check off" the condiments. His job involves accountability of all eleven condiments and also to determine if any new condiments on the table have a seal that hasn't been removed. Nothing infuriates an upperclassman more than trying to put ketchup on his food and nothing comes out because the plebe didn't take the seal off the new bottle. Finally, the plebes are responsible for cutting desserts to the exact number of pieces that correspond to the number of upperclassmen who desire the frippery. Therefore, if six cadets at the table want cake, then the plebe will cut the cake into exactly six pieces. Like all other pieces of food at the table, the cake is presented and then cut by the plebes. Once they have completed the cut, they pass the cake to the highest-ranking Cow for inspection. All these duties and many more are required before anyone, regardless of rank, can eat at the table. For the plebes, the faster they finish their job without any mistakes, the more time they have to eat their meal. This is undoubtedly the number one goal for the plebes. They know if the upperclassmen have food in their mouths, they won't be talking.

After finishing breakfast that morning, I stormed off in a hurry to finish preparing for all the exams I had throughout the day. My first test was from my Helicopter Design class and the second test was on Material Science. Both tests were coming from the Engineering Department, and I knew neither one was going to be easy. It was always funny taking a West Point test because they would always use scenarios that were applicable to the Army. For example, test questions at most colleges would involve finding the time train A met train B at point C, while a West Point test would involve finding the time that an F-22 jet met an Abrams tank at a location in Afghanistan. This kind of typical Army question would always make us laugh. After completing both exams that morning, I was happy with my performance. I was only concerned with a couple of answers, and that was usually a good sign. With the morning requirements complete, I headed to lunch formation and prepared my stomach for a tasty meal.

As I met my roommates, Jack and Mac, at formation, we discussed the eventful morning of tests and home-work. Needless to say, we weren't having the best day.

Jack, showing his frustration, made the comment, "I sure hope those plebes don't mess up their table duties because I'm really hungry."

Just as I was getting ready to respond, we heard the cadet regimental commander call the thousand cadets in our formation to attention.

After accountability was conducted, we marched into the mess hall and Jack and I continued our conversation.

Without missing a beat, Jack continued, "I mean, how long do you think it's going to take for them to learn to check the head of the table properly?"

"I don't know, it's starting to get a little ridiculous," I replied.

Over the last couple weeks, Jack was frustrated with the plebes' inability to cut the dessert and "check off" the head of the table. We knew how the plebes could fix the problem, but part of the process was letting them discov-er their own solutions to problems they encountered. By not giving the plebes a solution to their issues, it would help them develop qualities to become problem solvers instead of problem identifiers. Overhearing our conver-sation, a second-class cadet named Nick Horton chimed in on our discussion.

"All I got to say is we better get a lot of time to eat lunch today. I nearly split my chest open at the gym last night."

Horton was an atypical cadet who found his roots as a surfer from Satellite Beach, Florida. Unlike most laid-back surfers, Horton enjoyed bodybuilding while at the Academy, and his burly looks complimented his strong head ideology with plebes.

After the Poop Deck gave the command to take seats, the plebes at our table began working like bees at a hive. They needed to move fast and furious because if they didn't, they would face the wrath of the upperclassmen wanting to eat, especially CDT SGT Horton. The list of duties was long and full of minute details. While the freshmen waited for the food to arrive at the table, one plebe started announcing the drink for the meal. The plebe grabbed the large pitcher, which was already sitting on the table, and initiated the duties. He held the pitcher over his right shoulder and made an announcement to the table.

"Sir, the cold beverage for this meal is lemonade. Would anyone not care for lemonade, Sir?"

After the announcement, the plebe lowered the large pitcher to the table. As the plebe looked down the long table to hear the orders, he listened to the seven upperclassmen all say their preferences at the same time. Jack not only wanted some lemonade, but he only wanted four ice cubes in his drink. As the plebe listened to all the requests, I could see he was memorizing all the orders. For each mistake, it just further delayed the process of his ultimate goal: more time to eat. Once the plebe filled all the glasses and sent them down the table, the upperclassmen were relieved to see the plebe got every order correct.

While one plebe was pouring the glasses and sending them down the table, another plebe was dealing with the dreaded dessert. This was one of the duties that Jack and all the other upperclassmen were going to be watching closely due to the continued problems. The plebes struggled to find a solution to cutting the cake in odd numbers. When a person typically cuts a cake, he cuts it in half then cuts it into fourths, then eighths. The plebes never had a problem cutting the cake when they had those numbers to work with. The problem now was the upper class was purposefully changing their orders to make the plebes cut an odd number of slices. Therefore, when seven out of the ten cadets wanted to eat cake, the plebe would need to cut exactly 7 pieces at 51 degrees from the 360-degree cake.

Ready to start the duty, the plebe picked up the cake from the middle of the table and held it over his right shoulder and started with the memorized lines.

"Sir, the dessert for this meal is yellow cream pie. Would anyone not care for yellow cream pie, Sir?"

After the plebe's announcement, he would look down the table as three upperclassmen would undoubtedly always say they didn't care for dessert. As a result, this would leave the dreaded seven-piece cut. At first, a plebe's inclination is to say he doesn't care for any cake in order to reduce the number of slices to six pieces. Everyone knows it's much easier to cut the cake into six pieces rather than craftily cut the cake like a tool and dye maker into the exact number of seven. The decision not to eat dessert far outweighed the consequences of dealing with an upperclassman's creative ways of making him busy for a lousy cut on a seven-piece cake. This trick from the plebes would only work for a day before the upperclassmen would change the rules. Anytime this would happen, the upperclassmen would quickly fix the problem by having the plebes state their desire for cake prior to placing their own orders. This way, the upperclassmen would tailor their numbers to meet the golden seven-piece cut.

Looking down the table, I could see the plebe was putting the final touches on cutting the cake into seven pieces.

Upon completing the duty, the plebe announced to the table, "Sir, the cake has been cut. Dessert to Cadet Sergeant Horton for inspection please, Sir."

As the cake went up the table, CDT SGT Horton grabbed the cake and his face turned red. He always had the biggest blood vessel stick out on the side of his neck when he got angry.

"Wow, look at this piece right here. You see that? Why is this one so big?" Sergeant Horton questioned with beady eyes. After a couple seconds of silence, Horton said again, "Answer me, smacker. Why is this piece so big and this one so small?"

The plebe quickly answered back, "No excuse, Sir!"

Horton continued, "You better believe there's no excuse, but this leads me to an even more important question. Who at this table is getting the big piece?"

The plebe, not expecting that question, answered back, "Sergeant, the large piece is for you."

The plebe's response was obviously geared toward helping Horton get more food. He was hoping if he gave the large piece to the inspector that he might be merciful with his punishment.

CDT SGT Horton quickly fired back with his fist on the table, "Are you giving me the large piece because you think I'm fat? Is that what you think, smacker!"

"No, Sir," the plebe responded quietly.

Horton looked down at the cake and said, "I'll tell you what, smacker. Since you think I'm fat, I'm taking you to the gym tonight."

That was the end of the conversation as Horton flipped the cake to the table in disgust. At this point, I could tell Jack was getting more furious by the second. Hopefully, the plebes wouldn't make any more mistakes throughout the meal or Jack was going to lose his mind.

At this point, the waiter dropped off the food and the plebe sitting at the opposite end of the table started to announce the main dish. During the duties process, one plebe typically walked to the head of the table and checked off the condiments to see if they had accounted for the seals being removed. After ten seconds, the plebe standing beside Jack was obviously driving him crazy. Jack looked at the plebe and waited an additional five seconds before speaking.

"Are you ever going to get any faster at checking off the head of the table?" Jack questioned.

The plebe quickly responded but still didn't move. "Yes, Sir."

"How hard is it to count to eleven and develop a process to ensure all the seals are removed from the bottles? You could almost complete this duty from your seat on the other end of the table."

The plebe at this point quickly walked back to his seat and sat down. As the plebe sat down in his seat, we heard an announcement from the Poop Deck.

"Attention to orders."

During the middle of every meal, the school's adjutant makes an announcement to the Corps of Cadets. The plebes would always strive to complete their duties before this announcement took place. It was usually a good gauge to know if they did a good or poor job with their table duties. If they were fast, everyone at the table was eating before this announcement was conducted. Today wasn't one of those days; all the upperclassmen were still waiting to eat and half the lunchtime was already over.

Luckily for the plebes, a little West Point tradition lightened the mood at the table with the upperclassmen. As the announcement continued, we heard the adjutant say, "Please give your attention to the blood lady." I don't know when the ritual started, but West Point would constantly hold blood drives. They would get so many cadets to give blood that I think they had the date set on their calendars when our blood was ripe for picking. Well, anytime the Red Cross was visiting, the school would allow this "blood lady" to make an announcement during the middle of lunch to inform cadets they were back in

town. As a result, the Corps got in this habit of cheer-
ing so loud for the blood lady that she couldn't even hear
herself speak. The cheers and noise would continue until
she would give up and walk back down the steps from the
Poop Deck. The mess hall would sound like the crowd at
a Metallica concert, it was so loud. This day was no different than ones in the past because the upperclassmen
heard the announcement for the blood lady and everyone
started making an enormous racket until the poor blood
lady gave up. This might sound ridiculous and immature,
but this would literally bring so much joy to the entire
school. The little old blood lady probably thought we
were really rude, but the 95 percent turnout rate never
stopped her from coming back.

After the announcements were complete, the plebes
made their final memorized pronouncement.

"Sir, the fourth-class cadets at this table have performed their duties and are now prepared to eat."

Although the blood lady incident helped relieve some
of the odium Jack had for the plebes' inability to perform
duties, he quickly shouted, "Eat!"

About two minutes into the meal, Jack reached for
the ketchup and tried to put the tomato sauce on his
French fries. To his surprise, the seal underneath the
cap was still on the bottle. This was the last straw for
Jack and every other upperclassman at the table. Horton
started with reprimand for the plebe's failure to check off
the head of the table when he was interrupted by Jack.

"I'm not going to tolerate you plebes cutting the cake
like crap and checking off the head of the table for five
minutes and still making mistakes like this ketchup. You
need to figure this out by lunch tomorrow. You don't
want to see the result of failing to fix this problem."

Jack didn't raise his voice and spoke in a nonthreat-
ening manner. This usually scared plebes even more than
yelling and screaming. They knew that if the problem

wasn't fixed, there was going to be hell to pay.

The next day at lunch, we could tell CDT SGT Horton did a squat workout with the plebe who gave him the large piece of cake from the day before. It became obvious when he struggled to sit down in his chair.

As the plebes began their duties for the day, we had high expectations to see how they were going to correct their problems from the day before. While one of the plebes was busy filling the drinks, another one grabbed the carrot cake. Everyone at the table anxiously waited to see how the plebe was going to cut the cake today. After the plebe announced the dessert to the table, he did something that surprised everyone. After placing the cake back on the table, he took a small sugar packet and centered it on top of the cake. Once he got the sugar packet in the right position, he pulled out a small circular template and put it on top of the sugar packet. As everyone looked down the table, we could not believe our eyes. The plebe had made a template that showed him the exact places to mark the cake so he could cut it into the seven pieces that the upperclassmen requested. Once he made tick marks on the cake, he removed the sugar packet and template and cut the cake into seven perfect pieces. He was quick and very efficient. Before we could even comment on the plebe's great idea, he was sending the flawlessly cut cake to CDT SGT Horton for inspection.

As Horton took a close look at the cake, he smiled and commented, "Where's my big piece?"

By the look on the plebe's face, you could tell his sore body didn't enjoy the joke. Horton quickly continued, "Good work. This is the standard."

After the cake was inspected, it was time for one of the plebes to check off the head of the table. As the plebe walked towards our position, we could tell he was already counting the condiments to ensure no time was wasted. Once he stopped next to Jack's seat, he quickly glanced at all the bottles for less than five seconds and started walking away. We looked at the plebe like they couldn't be serious. We couldn't believe they had counted and checked for all the seals in less than five seconds.

Once the plebe returned to his seat, Jack said, "All right, how do you know all the seals are off the condiments?"

Without hesitation, the plebe responded, "Sir, we now make very small marks with knives on top of the lids to know if a bottle has been checked off. When I came to the head of the table, I already counted eleven bottles and all I needed to check was the mark on the lid."

Jack, nodding his head in approval, said, "Outstanding. There's always an easier way."

* * *

The BLUF of this story is leaders always find a more efficient and effective way to accomplish missions.

In the military, the duties of every organization are outlined by a Standard Operating Procedures (SOP) manual. This book provides the guidelines and fundamentals that describe every detail of how a unit should operate. Essentially, there are three ways leaders use the SOP. Poor leaders don't even read and know the regulations in the SOP that govern their unit. As one can imagine, it's very interesting to watch this leader take command of his Soldiers and give orders. Amateur leaders read their SOP and strictly believe there is no wiggle room for the precise words that define the book. They are the same individuals who refuse to accept any ideas that fall outside the guidelines of the information outlined by the SOP. Finally, you have experienced leaders. They view the SOP as a living, breathing document. They understand that the SOP is law, but they also understand warfare is constantly changing and demands leaders to always seek a better way to solve problems. These leaders will obey the lawful orders of the SOP and also submit changes and new ideas through their chain of command in order to improve existing doctrine for future leaders. These leaders adopt a principle that Thomas Edison is famous for stating: "We shall have no better conditions in the future if we are satisfied with all those which we have at present." Great leaders always question existing doctrine. They don't do this because they disagree with the way things are being done, but they do it because deep down inside they always think there's a better way to conduct business.

In the story, every upperclassman knew how to fix the problem the plebes were having at the table. We all had various techniques when we were plebes to perform duties in an expedient and efficient manner. To simply tell the plebes how to fix the problem defeats the purpose of lessons to be learned. At West Point, the last kind of environment we wanted to create was one in which people are only told what to do. Although the strict rules and regulations may appear to an outsider that this notion is not accurate, the truth is the institute breeds innovative thought. Upperclassmen would intentionally create an environment in which plebes must develop solutions to problems that appear indistinguishable. To their surprise, they would always find a better way to solve the problem regardless of their initial opinions.

The most important piece of the story is the sense of accomplishment that the plebes gained at the end of the story. Despite the lack of words expressed by the upperclassmen, they knew they had succeeded. In order for an individual to wholeheartedly believe the principle of this story, a connection must be made. I'm referring to a psychological connection that occurs between ideology and reinforced legitimacy. For example, when a person is told there's always an easier way to accomplish missions, the idea is typically perceived as platitude. This discernment is quickly viewed as fact once the individual experiences the success of his efforts for the first time. Over time, if an individual experiences success by creating innovative ways to successfully accomplish missions more efficiently, he will adopt the principle as truth opposed to counsel.

On June 2, 2001, I heard a speech given by Deputy Secretary of Defense Paul Wolfowitz at Michie Stadium. During the commencement speech to the graduating class, he discussed the importance of innovation and initiative by leaders to seek new ways of accomplishing future uncertainties. With the same responsibility that Jack ordered the plebes to find a new way to conduct business, the Deputy Secretary of Defense charged the graduating class of 2001 to fear complacency and become innovative. Ironically, less than three months after this speech, the World Trade Centers were destroyed and the graduating class found themselves implementing new ideas and methods of warfare against a terrorist enemy.

"This expectation of the familiar has gotten whole governments, sometimes whole societies, into trouble... I am told that in your time here, you grew accustomed to looking beyond the next parapet, to anticipate where you wanted to take this corps. You convinced your leaders to give you unprecedented authority in the day-to-day running of the corps. That kind of innovation and initiative are the keys to anticipating the unlikely and preparing for the unfamiliar, to being prepared to overcome the surprises that are almost inevitably going to come."
(Wolfowitz, 2001)

As Deputy Secretary Wolfowitz accurately predicted, the surprise inevitably came, but much faster than he or anyone else could have ever imagined. Most will agree the class of 2001 rose to the occasion. By heeding Deputy Secretary Wolfowitz' guidance, the lieutenants of the graduating class revamped an Army that wasn't prepared for the war that awaited. The graduates flawlessly helped refurbished a slow, cumbersome Army used to fight a massive front conflict into a quick, pliable force that can defeat a cellular enemy. If there is one thing the class of 2001 brought to the table upon graduation, it was their ability to always find a more efficient way to defeat their future adversaries.

11

The Autonomous Shadow

I was really nervous as I ran to the Engineering building from my room. I had been waiting for a couple weeks to find out my summer assignment, and this time I potentially had something to be excited about. Instead of hiking numerous miles in the woods with no food, I now had been at the Academy long enough to get an elective summer internship. The school called the program Academic Individual Advanced Development, or AIAD for short. Students from my class all had the opportunity to work in a civilian job that was related to our field of study. This was really going to be a nice break from the monotonous summers of military training. Once I arrived at the bulletin board where the internships were posted, I began running my finger down the list, looking for the last four of my social security number. This is how the school would always post grades or assignments. As I got to my number, it read:

8071 – National Aeronautical and Space Administration, Johnson Space Center, TX

As I read the paper, I literally jumped in the air because I got my number one choice. I was going to work at NASA in Houston, Texas. I hadn't been this excited in a very long time. Before the list came out, I was really nervous. Since there were only nineteen cadets in my entire year group who majored in Aerospace Engineering, the competition for summer jobs was very selective. Evidently, all my hours of studying had paid off. Hopefully, the opportunity would meet my enormous expectations.

As the academic year finished up, I quickly found myself on a flight to Houston. Lucky for me, the job at NASA was for two cadets, so I got to work with one of my best friends, Steve Crews. Before leaving, we had arranged to live on Galveston Beach and commute thirty minutes to work each day. Life couldn't have been better. Our free time was spent on the beach and our work time was spent working with astronauts all day. For two 21-year-old students, we couldn't have been afforded a better opportunity. No teachers, a great job, and the summer living on the beach. I knew many of our classmates would have been very jealous if they would have known about the job we had.

That summer, Steve and I got to meet some of the most incredible people. During our first week on the job, we were invited to the astronauts' flight briefing held on Tuesday morning. This was such an incredible experience because we got to sit in a room with well over fifty astronauts. During the briefing, they talked about numerous different topics that all related to flight safety and space equipment. After the briefing was complete, we were introduced to the astronauts in attendance. This was such an exciting experience for Steve and me because we had spent so much time studying the things they were "playing with" on a daily basis.

Of all the astronauts, there were two men in the room who were getting a lot of attention from all the other members of this elite group. Steve and I looked at our supervisor and asked her why they were so popular.

She said, "Oh, those two guys just got back from space two weeks ago. They had been living on the International Space Station for the last six months."

Needless to say, we were star struck. For me, this was much more impressive than meeting any celebrity or pro athlete. These men were truly American heroes. As the crowd of astronauts dissipated from the two men who just returned to earth a couple of weeks ago, Steve and I made our way to where they were standing.

As we approached the two men, our supervisor introduced us as students from West Point who were working at NASA for the summer. Expecting a subtle smile and courteous hello, we got the opposite. Astronaut Colonel (COL) Carl Walz gazed at us with as much excitement as we showed toward him.

Before we could even introduce ourselves, he started the conversation and said, "Hey, guys. How would you like to come over to my house and have dinner?"

Steve and I, completely astounded, looked at each other in disbelief and responded in unison with a "Yes, Sir!" We couldn't believe that the first words of our conversation were, "Would you like to have dinner?"

As we continued to talk, COL Walz indicated that his son was interested in attending West Point, so he figured it would be a great opportunity for everyone to have a good meal and share stories. *What an opportunity!* Steve and I were invited to have dinner with the man who just broke the United States space flight endurance record. He just returned from spending 196 days in space 2 weeks ago and wanted to have dinner with us.

The next night, Steve and I found ourselves driving to COL Walz' house for dinner. We were very nervous and didn't want to poorly represent ourselves or our school. On our way to his house, Steve suggested that we stop and buy a bottle of wine as a gift for having us over. After a quick debate over whether it was an appropriate gift, we decided to go with the wine due to a lack of options.

As we got to his house, we were welcomed as if we had known his family our entire lives. We were overjoyed with such a unique opportunity that we almost forgot to give his wife the bottle of wine. They could tell we were nervous, but they calmed our anxiety once dinner started and we started sharing stories. Steve and I were obviously not interested in telling stories about West Point, but I'm sure the Walz family wasn't interested in telling more space stories either. Despite our hidden aversion for our own stories, we began sharing our experiences with each other.

I initiated the volley of questions by asking COL Walz what it was like sleeping in space for six months. At first, he laughed and said that it was something that a lot of people forgot about. He said it was difficult at first to get used to and that most astronauts would slumber in sleeping bags that were attached to the walls of the International Space Station (ISS). He said pillows would stay in place with Velcro. Although pillows weren't needed, it was hard for most newbies to get used to sleeping without the staple item. He said that after a couple months, his body became accustomed to the weightlessness and he occasionally slept without the sleeping bag. After hearing the story, my mind began to wonder.

I questioned further about how that was even possible. In response, he continued by saying that once he was done working, he would just fall asleep in mid-air. Evidently, without gravity pulling his arms down, he looked like a zombie floating around the station throughout the night. He said without the sleeping bag, he would sometimes wake up in different nodes of the ISS. This, among many other stories, kept Steve and I glued to COL Walz' dinner table like we were watching an action thriller all night.

The next day at work proved to be equally exciting. Thanks to COL Walz and our supervisor, they had arranged for us to spend the day with COL Jerry Ross. This was such an exciting experience because he showed

us around some of the most exciting places that Johnson
Space Center has to offer. COL Ross was the first human
to enter space seven times. Steve and I continued to be
astounded by the caliber of people who went well out of
their way to show us some of the most interesting things
our country has developed over the years.

After touring the Neutral Buoyancy Lab (NBL),
where the astronauts train in the world's largest pool, we
were introduced to NASA's Reduced Gravity Office. Although the pool was very impressive, the Reduced Gravity program was one of the most astounding things I saw
all summer. We were introduced to the program director, Mr. John Yaniec. He was the individual responsible for test coordination aboard the KC-135 "weightless
wonder." Although this is the official nickname for the
aircraft, everyone else referred to the plane as the "vomit
comet." After talking with Mr. Yaniec, he said the purpose of the vomit comet was to provide researchers and
astronauts with an environment that can provide zero
gravity for 30 second intervals. The aircraft was capable
of producing this reduced gravity by nose-diving the aircraft from 40,000 feet to 10,000 feet while flying over
the Gulf of Mexico. The experience sounded exhilarating.
Without hesitation, Steve and I asked Mr. Yaniec what we
needed to do to get a ride on this remarkable aircraft.

Laughing, Mr. Yaniec said, "You need to have a purpose to fly on the aircraft. You just can't fly because you
want to have fun."

As we continued to ask more questions, Mr. Yaniec
informed us of a program that NASA offers to college students. If students are interested in flying a project or experiment on the KC-135, they can submit an application
to the Reduced Gravity Office. If the scientist/engineers
at NASA are interested in the idea, they would fly the
student(s) back to Houston to test the idea in the vomit
comet. For me, I had never been more motivated.

After hearing Mr. Yaniec, I quickly responded, "OK, so if I come up with a project of interest, I can come back here and fly in this aircraft?"

Smiling and handing me his business card, Mr. Yaniec responded, "You sure can. You just need a purpose to fly in this aircraft."

From that point on, a purpose was all I sought. I needed to think of an idea that wasn't so lofty that I couldn't complete it, but important enough that NASA would want to test my project/idea. So I began to brainstorm different concepts. I asked the numerous astronauts I worked with on a daily basis if there was anything they really needed in space. Although they provided great feedback, I really didn't get any ideas I was capable of producing. After a week of getting nowhere, I began to doubt my ability to pull off such a lofty goal.

Not only did I lack a feasible idea, but I didn't even know if I could get the faculty at West Point to fund and support a capstone project that was outside the curriculum. Before leaving for the summer, I had already been assigned to a senior project that had me designing and building a miniature unmanned aerial flying vehicle that could be used as reconnaissance. Even if I did come up with a great idea to fly on the vomit comet, I would have to brief all the heads of the Engineering Department in order to get the funds and resources to develop something in less than a year. Additionally, I would need to get West Point to fund my return to NASA for testing. After contemplating all the issues, reality was starting to set in.

Instead of belaboring the idea, I grabbed a beer from the fridge, a lawn chair, a towel, some chips, and my wallet and headed out for the beach. As I got out of the elevator at our hotel and walked off the deck, I was carrying so much stuff that I felt like the tips of my fingers were going to fall off. My knuckles were white and the pain in my cramped hands was making my feet scamper faster. The items in my hands were slowly creeping their way toward the ground as my scamper turned into a run. I only had another forty feet to the beach when the chair and chips slipped out of my hand and onto the ground. I naturally saved the beer from falling because this was clearly a priority. By saving the beer, the price I paid was a bag of chips that was all over the ground. Completely frustrated, I took a quick break and grabbed my chair and the ripped bag of empty potato chips and continued my scamper to my spot on the beach. As I put all my belongings in their final resting spot, I looked back at where I dropped my chips and saw a bunch of seagulls swooping in for the food. As I stared at the circling seagulls, I was endowed with a miraculous idea. *This was it!* Even though I had no chips to eat, the terrible event gave me my purpose. I was motivated yet again.

The next day, I went to work and couldn't wait to ask some questions to the brilliant people I got to work with. I asked multiple astronauts if they often found themselves short of hands while operating inside the International Space Station. Without any argument, they all agreed that some extra arms would be useful. They said that many times they would be working on multiple projects and mission-essential tools or equipment would float away if bumped or lightly touched. After hearing this information, I knew my idea was going to be the perfect project to get a flight in the KC-135.

At the end of the exciting and fun-filled summer, I returned to West Point for the start of my senior year. I was now a Firstie and things were supposed to be much easier than the previous three years. Although this was my expectation, my year ended up being one of the most difficult years due to self-induced extra work. Instead of living in the company, I was chosen to fill a job on the Brigade staff as the officer in charge of drill and ceremony. I moved from the building I had been living in for the last two years and was now going to spend the semester with a new roommate I didn't know. I was excited to be given so much responsibility, but I wasn't happy about living away from all my friends.

On the first day back, I met my new roommate, Matt Parretti. I recognized Matt from some of my classes a few years back, but I really didn't know him very well. Together, Matt and I were responsible for the drill and ceremony of the entire school. It was a huge undertaking getting our 4,000 classmates and underclassmen to practice marching around the parade field for hours on end. Before classes even started on our first day back, I was already working hard at my computer putting concept sketches together for my idea to get back to NASA. It was a bold undertaking, but I was determined to see it through. As I worked diligently at my computer, Matt watched curiously as he jammed away on his acoustic guitar. Typically, this might have distracted me, but I was so focused on this idea I got from the dropped potato chips that his version of Bon Jovi didn't even make me flinch. After a couple hours went by, Matt stopped playing and interrupted my work.

He said, "Preston, I know I don't know you very well, but what the hell are you doing? We haven't even started class yet and it looks like you're trying to dismantle nuclear weapons over there."

Matt was one of the most laid-back people I had ever seen and I suspected that my diligent typing was taking away from the aura in the room that he was trying to create.

As I stopped typing on my computer and turned around, I told him, "OK, I'll tell you, but you have to promise not to laugh."

Shaking his head a little bit, Matt said, "I'm not going to laugh. I just can't understand why you're studying when we don't have class for a week."

So I answered his question with trepidation because I knew it was such a lofty goal. I told him that I had worked at NASA over the summer and that I was designing a project to get a flight in the KC-135 vomit comet. After I completed my quick pitch, Matt reacted in a manner opposite of what I expected. Instead of making fun of my idea, he became truly interested in how it worked.

As the week progressed, Matt could tell I was working very hard on developing a proposal for the heads of the Mechanical Engineering Department. Despite my diligent work, he put equal attention into strumming his guitar. I knew he was from New Jersey, so maybe that's why he was so obsessed with Bon Jovi. Matt, watching me pour every ounce of time and energy into my project, put down his guitar and interrupted me once again.

He said, "Preston, you know you're going to need a lot of electronics and computer code in order create that thing you're designing."

A little frustrated with the negative energy, I responded, "Yeah, you're right, I probably will."

Although I didn't know it at the time, Matt was a genius. At first glance, he looked like a laid-back cadet who probably would rather play his guitar than study for his next exam. To my surprise, he was being considered for the Hertz Fellowship Master's Scholarship and did everything to keep the smart, geeky image under wraps. At this point in our relationship, I didn't know any of that about Matt. As I turned back around to continue typing on my computer, he began to speak again.

Matt said, "Well, if you're looking for an electrical engineer and a computer programmer, I know some really smart people who might be interested in working with you."

Pausing for a second and turning back around, I looked at Matt and said, "Oh, yeah? Who's that?"

He continued, "Well, for starters, I could be one of your electrical engineers. Also, I know two other guys who are really smart. I'm sure if we sat down and talked over the project, they'd be more than interested. By the way, it would probably help when you brief the department heads of your idea if you have a team already assembled. This will show them that you're organized and have a solid plan in place."

Thinking briefly about Matt's advice, I couldn't argue with his proposal. He could tell that I was a little hesitant to approve of their implementation because I didn't know his friends.

As I continued to ponder the proposition, Matt continued, "I'll tell you what. I'll give them a call and we'll meet after dinner tonight. If you're not interested, no big deal. We all have senior capstone projects that we're already assigned, so we'll just continue down that path."

After a little hesitation, I said, "All right, give them a call. We'll chat after dinner."

After dinner, Matt and his two friends stopped by our room. We had just finished a Thursday-night dinner, so everyone was still dressed in their white-over-gray uniforms. Matt and his friends gathered around my desk to hear about my idea to fly in the vomit comet. As I looked up at Matt and his friends, my eyes about popped out of my head.

One of the cadet medals that the school awards for academic excellence is a gold star with wreath. Not many cadets get to wear this award because it's only awarded to individuals who have an overall GPA of 3.67 or higher. Essentially, a cadet needs to have a straight "A" average in order to wear this medal on his uniform. Less than 10 percent of cadets are ever awarded this honor. So, when I looked up from my desk and saw my roommate with his two friends all wearing gold stars, I couldn't believe my eyes. Matt and his two friends were three of the smartest guys in my entire class.

My trepidation toward implementing them into the project quickly turned to equanimity. Seeing the three of them standing in front of my desk, my eyes projected disbelief.

I looked at Matt and said, "Wow, you weren't kidding when you said you had smart friends."

Matt just laughed and said, "Tell them what you're doing. They're going to love this."

As I started explaining the project to Matt's friends, they grew more and more excited and interested with each and every sentence. They thought the idea was going to be very difficult, but they were confident they'd be able to design their respective portions of the deal. At the end of my pitch, they all wanted in. I looked at Matt's first friend, Shawn Lough, who was an electrical engineer.

He could sense I wanted to hear input, but instead, he looked at me and said, "Sign me up. Everything you've talked about looks awesome."

Next, a guy named Brock Hershberger, who was going to be the computer programmer, said, "Sounds good to me."

Finally, I looked at Matt and he said, "It looks like we got ourselves a team."

I couldn't believe it. Everything was really starting to come together. Not only was my proposal for the Engineering Department looking better, but now I had a team comprised of really smart engineers.

Later that week, the head of the Mechanical Engineering Department decided to meet with me to discuss my proposal. I was very excited that a Colonel would take time out of his busy day to hear a young cadet's ideas. As I entered his office, there was a Lieutenant Colonel and a doctor sitting in his office. I had prepared my briefing in a small binder that I put in front of his desk.

He said, "All right, Cadet Pysh. What do you have

for me?" I had rehearsed the proposal numerous times in my room. There was nothing going to stand in my way. I started off strong and confident.

"Sir, I had the unique opportunity to work at Johnson Space Center this summer and I was introduced to the Reduced Gravity program. Most recognize this program for the KC-135 aircraft, better known as the vomit comet. The aircraft is a test bed that provides weightlessness. The aircraft allows NASA to test space equipment and train astronauts. After talking with the flight director at the Reduced Gravity Office, he informed me of an opportunity to return and test an experiment if I could develop something that was worthy of testing. As a result, I have developed an idea that I call the Autonomous Shadow. The concept is simple: I want to build a small space vehicle that can follow astronauts around inside the International Space Station without any assistance. After talking with numerous astronauts, they assured me this vehicle would be very useful to keep accountability of mission-essential equipment. For example, if you were an astronaut and wanted to have a video camera follow you around in the space station while you conducted experiments, you could attach the camera to the Autonomous Shadow's payload. As a result, your every move could be recorded without having to touch a button."

As I continued to explain the aspects of the project, I could tell the Colonel and his team of professors were becoming more interested in my idea. I had concept sketches and numerous different proposals on how the engineering design could be accomplished. After my briefing was complete, the Colonel began asking questions.

"So, how do you propose the vehicle will move in the space station?"

Without hesitation, I responded, "Sir, although we still need to implement the entire engineering design process to arrive at the most suitable solution, we are strongly considering using pneumatic jets combined with ultrasonic sensors."

Hearing my answer, the Colonel could tell that I paid attention last semester. One of the most fundamental steps that we learned in the design process was that all options need to be ascertained before decisive conclusions were made. After the first question, numerous others followed. I could tell they were trying to dig as deep as they could before hitting questions that didn't have answers. Following the barrage of questions, which I felt were all answered appropriately, the Colonel concluded the meeting.

He said, "Preston, I can see you've worked very hard and have given this a lot of thought, but right now all our faculty has been assigned to the other capstone projects. You would need to find a professor who would be willing to work overtime to support your project."

Completely disappointed, I slowly lowered my head.

As the room quickly went silent, I heard the doctor standing at the side of the Colonel's desk say, "Sir, I'd love to be Cadet Pysh's advisor on this project."

Without hesitation, the Colonel continued, "Well, I guess that was easy enough. I'll initially designate $1,600 to this project and we'll see what you can come up with. Good luck!"

Before I could even say thank you, the Colonel was getting out of his chair. I quickly jumped to attention and rendered a salute. *I did it!*

I convinced the Engineering Department to let me design a space vehicle for the International Space Station. As I walked out of the room, the generous doctor introduced himself. His name was Dr. Leemie and he was very young looking. He looked like a 22-year-old student, but had already acquired his doctorate and was a professor within the department. Dr. Leemie immediately started talking business.

"I know you just briefed the Colonel that you want to design this vehicle to travel in three dimensions, but that is way too lofty of a goal. You only have eight months to get something working, so you need to make this thing travel on one axis before going any further. If you can do that, you'll get your ride in the vomit comet."

As we continued to talk, he described many different aspects that I hadn't considered. This young doctor was clearly thinking on a level that far exceeded my capacity. After hearing many of his ideas, I became more excited because I now had another brilliant mind to add to the team.

As the months progressed, the Autonomous Shadow began to take shape. There were numerous requirements and gates that we needed to meet in order to develop a working model. At the end of the design process, we decided to model the vehicle to look like a thick circular cake. Inside the "cake" would be the compressed air tanks, electronics, pneumatic tubes, regulators, valves, and all sorts of mechanics to give the vehicle life. The top and bottom of the "cake" was going to be the payload for the astronauts to attach their mission equipment. This is the area where they could Velcro a laptop, video camera, or any other tools that were deemed necessary for a mission. Once the Autonomous Shadow vehicle was turned on, the astronauts could set the standoff distance they wanted the vehicle to stay from their changing position. Once that standoff was sent, they could ignore the vehicle and the tools they would attach. After the short setup, the Autonomous Shadow would follow their every move. The design process was long and arduous, but at the end of the development, we were confident our design would work. Now that our calculations and sketches were complete, it was time to start building the vehicle.

As our team started construction, we encountered numerous roadblocks along the way. I had the privilege of working with a faculty member whose specific job was helping cadets fabricate their capstone projects. His name was Jeff Butler, and he had plenty of experience dealing with Engineering students and their designs. Mr. Butler truly added a lot to the project because he was the bridge between concepts and reality. He and I were designing all the hardware while Shawn, Brock, and Matt were working on the circuit board and software programming. It was such a unique experience to see all the angles of the project come together. One of the most difficult obstacles that our team had to overcome was developing a way to test the vehicle before hopefully getting it flown in Houston. It was obviously difficult, considering there weren't many ways to simulate zero gravity.

In order to test the vehicle, Mr. Butler and I thought the best approach would be to build an air table over which the vehicle could hover. It would be the equivalent of an air hockey table, only the vehicle would be the puck. As the vehicle would hover, we could then test the intelligence of the vehicle to remain a designated distance from a body. Although this would have been the optimal test bed for the vehicle, we weren't able to implement this idea because we lacked the funds and time to design, build, and implement a large "hockey table" capable of producing enough airflow to lift the relatively heavy Autonomous Shadow.

A few weeks later, Mr. Butler and I were starting to put the final touches on the vehicle when we started talking.

He said, "You know, I think I found a solution to our testing problem."

Very interested in how Mr. Butler planned on simulating zero gravity, I said, "Oh, yeah? What's that?"

He continued, "I think if we put the vehicle on a raft and place it in a large pool of calm water, you'd see it move just like zero gravity. It would obviously move slower due to the drag in the water, but that's something you guys could calculate and account for."

He was right. We could use a pool of water as a test bed. That was going to work; what a great idea.

That night, I went back to my room and calculated the amended numbers that the nozzles would have to fire in order to move the vehicle on a raft in water. After figuring out the new times, I gave Brock a call so he could adjust the programming code. The team quickly adapted to the change and we were back in business, ready to test the vehicle.

As testing began, the vehicle was working great. We didn't have much time between the testing and the deadline to have our products sent to West Point and NASA. Our proposal was almost 200 pages of information supporting the flight safety and applicability of the vehicle. NASA was very concerned about putting a vehicle in the KC-135 aircraft because it carried a small tank with 20,000 pounds/in² of compressed air. We had coordinated with the engineers of the tank and regulators to ensure a large margin of safety was associated with the tank and all its components. The formalities and precautions were things that I had never learned in the classroom, so getting this experience firsthand was invaluable. Our team had traveled down a long path to completion, but eventually we had finalized our proposal and vehicle before NASA's deadline. As we sent our massive packet of information to the Reduced Gravity Office in Houston, we anxiously awaited a response. We had dedicated hundreds of hours to this project, and our ticket to ride on the KC-135 was now at NASA's discretion. Even though we had mitigated all the risks involved with the pressurized air tank, the vehicle could still be unfit for flight. Our fingers were crossed.

It was a week later and we still hadn't heard anything from NASA on the project's approval to fly. As we anxiously awaited a response, things started looking worse. I got a call from our supervisor, Dr. Leemie, and he told me that I needed to come by his office to talk about the specifics of our project. Immediately, I was concerned. He didn't sound very upbeat on the phone, so I was anticipating terrible news. As I got in his office, I sat down and he began to talk.

He said, "Preston, the department is concerned about the amount of time you'll be missing classes if you go to Houston to test your project. Right now, if your project is even approved by NASA, you'll miss an entire week of class. That's a lot of makeup work!"

Hearing his concern instantly made my hopes of accomplishing my goal start to fade. He was right. How in the world was I going to complete a week's worth of classes and run all the tests on the Autonomous Shadow in Houston?

After a long pause, I looked up at Dr. Leemie and said, "I'll come up with a plan and make this work."

After hearing my response, he said, "All right. It needs to be good, because the only person who can approve you missing that many classes is the Dean of the school."

I paused for a brief second, looked down at the ground, realizing this was going to be difficult, and said, "I'll make it happen."

I walked out of Dr. Leemie's office and ran back to my room to call the team. Brock, Shawn, Matt, and I all got together in my room and devised a plan to "make it happen." We started contacting all our instructors and getting a signed report of our current grades. We wrote out courses of action pertaining to how our homework and tests could be rescheduled. Essentially, we developed yet another proposal on how we were capable of missing so much school while testing our project in Houston.

The next week, Dr. Leemie informed me that the

Dean was hesitant to approve our trip to Houston. Evidently, after much persuasion from a certain Colonel within the Engineering Department, the Dean signed off on the trip. I was thrilled to hear the great news, but I was almost positive that Shawn, Brock, and Matt's perfect grades probably helped us all get to Houston.

Some say lightning doesn't strike twice in the same spot, but later that same day, I got another phone call. When I answered the phone, the gentleman on the other end introduced himself as a doctor from Johnson Space Center. The gentleman said he was the reviewing officer for the Autonomous Shadow proposal and wanted to call and congratulate our team. He said our team's proposal was approved and he found our work very intriguing. The conversation was concise yet electrifying, as I attempted to control my utter excitement. After hanging up the phone with the doctor, I let out the biggest scream. I had accomplished my goal and was going to experience floating in zero gravity firsthand.

As I quickly caught myself daydreaming, I jumped off the bed and ran for the phone. I almost broke the numbers on the dial pad as I called my three teammates. We had pulled it off, we had secured our seat, or should I say, "air," in the KC-135. I had finally developed "a purpose" to fly in the vomit comet.

Within a couple weeks, Brock, Shawn, Matt, and I were on a flight for Houston. We had successfully met all the gates and requirements and were now going to test the Autonomous Shadow at Johnson Space Center. After meeting numerous points of contact from my previous summer's internship, I informed them that I was returning to test an experiment in the KC-135. Instantly, my summer colleagues were willing to introduce the team to more astronauts and give them a thorough tour of the center during our time off. It was exciting getting to talk to astronauts Colonel Patrick Forrester and Colonel

William "Bill" McArthur, because they were West Point graduates.

COL McArthur informed the four of us that he flew gold from our class rings into space last year. He said it was part of a program in which families of deceased graduates donated their class rings to the newly graduating class. After the rings were donated, COL McArthur took the nostalgic rings into space and then melted them upon his return. It was this melted gold that was added to our class rings before they were cast and given to our class the previous fall. After hearing the story from COL McArthur, all four of us looked down at our rings and couldn't believe the story we had heard. We had no idea some of the gold used for our rings was worn by former graduates and flown in space. What an incredible program. We all held our heads a little higher after talking to these esteemed graduates.

Although we spent a little of our free time talking to the astronauts and touring the space center, most of the time was spent taking care of business. We had to attend two days of training before being allowed to get our flight on the vomit comet. At the end of the second day of classes, we had to complete training in an altitude pressure chamber. The purpose of the training was to teach us the symptoms of hypoxia. The experience was actually really fun. Before entering the chamber, the four of us were all handed a written exam. We were instructed not to look at the questions until the chamber director gave us the signal to do so. As we entered the small room, we were ordered to don our oxygen masks. After everyone's mask was secure, the director signaled to someone outside the chamber to start reducing the pressure in the room. By lowering the pressure there was a lot less oxygen in the chamber, which simulated flying at a high altitude without oxygen. Although we didn't realize the effects of reduced oxygen to the brain, we were about to find out. After a few minutes, the chamber was depressurized and the director gave us the signal to take off our masks.

For the first couple seconds, everything seemed normal. After getting our masks off, the director ordered us to begin taking our written tests. As I flipped over the exam, I looked at the first five questions and they were all elementary math problems. None of the problems were harder than adding or subtracting. After about the fifth problem, I looked up to see how everyone else in the chamber was doing on the test. Everyone looked busy filling out the answers, so I went back to work. As I looked back at the page, the questions seemed harder. The test read, "Name a state that begins with a 'C.'" *Oh, wow,* I thought to myself. *There aren't many states that begin with 'C.'* I skipped that question and went for the next. "Who is the current Vice President of the United States?" *Oh, I know that one too, but wow...um, I wonder what everyone else is doing?* I looked around the chamber and everyone looked like zombies. I felt like someone had flipped me upside down and dumped my brain out. I barely remember the director instructing me to put my mask back on. Within seconds of getting the oxygen mask back on my face, I instantly regained consciousness with reality.

Looking across the chamber, I watched the director tell Brock to re-don his mask. Matt, Shawn, and everyone else in the chamber already had their masks back on their faces. Everyone was back from the strange mindless journey except Brock. As we watched the director instruct Brock yet again, he just nodded his head in understanding, but lacked the smarts to put the mask back on his face. After the director instructed Brock yet a third time, he realized the only way it was getting back on his face was with some assistance. As Brock and the director got his mask back on his face, a couple seconds passed and he was already back to normal. At the conclusion of our time in the pressure chamber, we all got out and teased Brock about being too brainless to re-don his mask. Brock didn't hesitate to return the banter as he reviewed our written tests. After looking at Matt's test, Brock said, "Paretti, according to this test, your mother's maiden name is President Bush." As we all laughed at each other's stupidity in the chamber, we all had a profound appreciation for the importance of oxygen levels at higher elevations.

After completing all the classes, tests, and the altitude chamber, our team was ready to take flight. As we loaded the Autonomous Shadow into the large KC-135, excitement filled the fuselage. The aircraft had been completely retrofitted to support an out-of-earth experience. All the seats in the aircraft were removed and the walls were padded. Before the aircraft took off, we rehearsed our testing numerous times. We were very concerned that our lack of experience with floating would interrupt our testing of the Shadow. After talking to Mr. Yaniec, the flight director, he said that many people have a hard time focusing once they start to float. Based on his recommendation, our team diligently rehearsed every step of our experiment.

Within an hour of our launch, we had an unexpected visitor come to the aircraft to wish us luck. It was Astronaut COL Forrester, who we met during the previous day. The airfield was a few miles from his office, so when we saw he made the trip to our location, we were very excited. A new level of motivation was brought to the team as we got our pictures with him and the Autonomous Shadow while standing inside the KC-135.

It was time. We were inside the windowless KC-135 as the main door closed and we could feel the aircraft begin to taxi. I was very nervous about getting sick because I didn't want my weak stomach to ruin the adventure of a lifetime. In just a small amount of time, we could feel the aircraft lift off the ground and take flight. It was very strange being in a large commercial-sized aircraft and lying on the floor during takeoff with no seat belt. It took about 15 minutes for the plane to reach its intended destination over the Gulf of Mexico before performing its 30,000-foot plunge toward the earth. As the flight director, John Yaniec, started to count, we knew the first dive was about to occur.

"Three, two, one, here we go!" Mr. Yaniec shouted.

As I heard him say, "Here we go," my body slowly lifted off the floor where I was sitting.

I felt like the prop in a magic show that was miraculously floating before the eyes of an astounded audience. As I sat weightless in midair like a genie hovering over a blanket, I looked at a bottle of water that Shawn had been drinking before takeoff. He had finished half the water, but now I was looking at the bottle suspended in midair with the half-drank water not sitting at the bottom of the bottle. Instead, the water was floating around inside of the bottle with no direction or purpose. Everything Mr. Yaniec had described before launch was coming true. Shawn and I were losing focus of the project due to the surreal circumstances.

As we simultaneously realized that we weren't staying focused on the experiment, Shawn said, "All right, we better get this thing started."

As we finally tethered ourselves back to the floor to start testing, we heard Mr. Yaniec shout, "Get your feet on the ground. We are coming out!"

Within a second of hearing his voice, it felt like someone dropped an elephant on my back. I looked down the fuselage of the aircraft as everyone and everything came crashing back to the padded floor. We were floating for approximately 30 seconds before the pilot had to recover the aircraft and initiate a sharp climb back to 40,000 feet. During the climb we experienced 2Gs of force for

1 minute and 30 seconds. We had gone from zero gravity to double our weight in a matter of seconds. As we patiently waited for the next dive, there was no break or time to reconsider our decisions to fly on the aircraft. As the aircraft acquired the 40,000 feet yet again, the aircraft immediately initiated another dive. The pilot flying the aircraft was relentless on the individuals with weak stomachs.

On the second plummet, Shawn and I were prepared to begin our tests. It was very difficult to remain focused as we calculated the vehicle's speed between checkpoints. We floated alongside the Autonomous Shadow, measuring the times it took to travel between predetermined distances. The purpose of our research was twofold. First, we wanted to validate the vehicle's ability to maintain standoff from our simulated astronaut body. Second, we wanted to optimize the programming code that dictated the vehicle's movement.

After about 25 dives in the KC-135, Shawn and I had collected all the data we needed for the experiment. In an effort to enjoy our remaining zero-gravity dives, we secured the Autonomous Shadow to the floor and prepared to have fun. As we were experiencing the 2G climb back to 40,000 feet, Shawn shouted to the flight director.

"Hey, Sir. During the next dive, can you spin me in a circle?"

Without any hesitation, Mr. Yaniec replied, "Sure thing. Just float over here once we start the dive."

As we reached the top of the parabola, Shawn and I lifted off the ground and floated our way to Mr. Yaniec's position. As Shawn approached the flight director's location, he was directed to curl up into a ball. Once Shawn complied with his order, Mr. Yaniec gently grabbed his folded arms and lightly pushed him head over heels. As Shawn started doing summersaults in midair, Mr. Yaniec didn't touch his body again after the initial push. As I floated beside Shawn and Mr. Yaniec, I could see Shawn continued to do summersaults without any more assistance. I literally witnessed Newton's first law of motion firsthand: "A body persists its state of rest or uniform motion unless acted upon by an external unbalanced force." *What an awesome sight!*

During the next dive, Shawn and I wanted to get a picture of the unique experience. Before our flight departed that morning, we had made a poster from a piece of cardboard that we wanted in the photograph. After positioning ourselves like Superman in midair with the poster held in front of our faces, we each got individual pictures to show our families.

At the conclusion of our team's trip to NASA, we had incredible stories to tell. I chose to tell my story a little differently than my teammates. Instead of just telling friends and family, I contacted my hometown newspaper to write a story about our team's project. I told the reporter that I had something very special that I was hoping she could run on the cover of the next week's newspaper. After the reporter read my story and saw the pictures, she decided to run the story.

It was 11 May 2003 when my mother walked out of her house and down to the mailbox at the end of the driveway. As she reached in the mailbox and pulled out the newspaper, she was shocked and surprised. Along with a full article about the Autonomous Shadow project was a front-page, 8x10 picture of me floating with a cardboard sign that read, "Happy Mother's Day from zero gravity."

* * *

The BLUF of this story has two learning points. First, always surround yourself with people you admire. Second, setting goals and expressing them to close friends and family provides a conduit for accomplishing your aspirations.

My father always told me not to run with dogs because I'd get fleas. This statement is so true and should never be treated as a cliché. I was never the smartest kid in class, but I always surrounded myself with people I admired. The only reason I was able to earn a flight on the KC-135 was due to having exceptional friends and faculty. After hearing the basic details of this project, anyone reading the story can tell the Autonomous Shadow project was a huge undertaking. It was only accomplished because of the caliber of people working on my team. Shawn, Brock, and Matt truly were some of the smartest individuals I've ever worked with. By surrounding myself with friends who I respected on a personal and academic level, I was capable of achieving goals well outside my scholastic means.

The by-product of associating with individuals you respect is it provides motivation to emulate their character or behavior. This simple fact is very important to ponder because heroes and admirable public figures have increasingly become twisted in modern society. Choosing the right role models is more important now than ever before. Instead of parents encouraging their children to honor/respect intelligent teachers in school, they now promote their children to emulate the behaviors of Hollywood celebrities who use drugs and live dysfunctional lives. In an effort to promote these false idols, parents attend school board meetings concerned about multi-million-dollar sports complexes instead of new academic programs. Surrounding yourself with admirable people can have a disparaging impact if the word "admirable" is used in the wrong context. For example, do you admire the sports star because he can make a lot of money by hitting baseballs, or do you admire the athlete because he gives back to the local community and is a philanthropist? As one might suspect, it is very important to fully comprehend why a "hero" is considered admirable. Surrounding yourself with the wrong "admirable" people will always have contradictory expectations.

If you were to ever open my wallet, you would find a small piece of paper inside that lists five short-term and five long-term goals I want to complete. I've found that when goals are physically established on a piece of paper, the chances of accomplishing those aspirations increase exponentially. People tend to go through life with no goals or purpose and as a result, they have no accomplishments. Think about things from your own perspective. What long-term goals do you have? Before reading any further, put this book down and really think about that question. Can you think of five long-term objectives that you desire? Now, instead of thinking about it, I challenge you to pull out a small piece of paper and list five short-term and five long-term goals. If you are the person who kept reading without actually writing, you're probably the same person who wonders why your goals never materialize. This simple exercise of listing your own expectations provides a roadmap to progress. Remember, it's only a dream until you write it down, then it becomes a goal. You'll be amazed at how well it works!

Over the years, I've had friends fetch money out of my wallet and come across the little page listing my goals. Immediately, it tends to be fodder for satire. I've never let the jokes bother my ambitions. In fact, I find it helps to materialize my objectives. Mark Twain said, "Keep away from people who try to belittle your ambitions. Small people always do that, but the really great make you feel like you, too, can become great." By telling close friends and family about goals and ambitions, you will initiate prospects for achievement. This is a scary thought for most people because they fear failure and what others might think. That is a common feeling and it should be expected, but at the same time, this fear is useful. This fear can be harnessed into motivation to complete your goals. No one ever said it better than the famous sculptor, Michelangelo, who said, "The greatest danger for most of us is not that our aim is too high and we miss it, but that it is too low and we reach it."

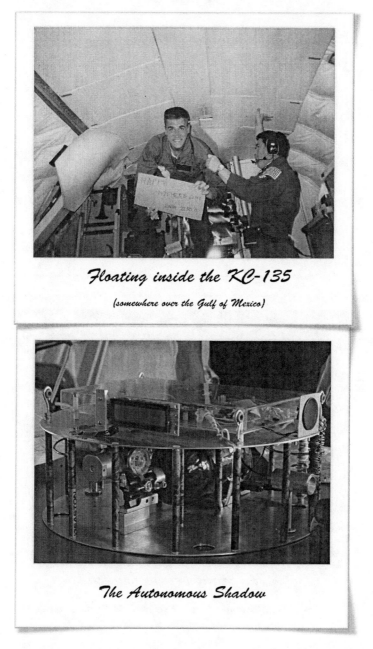

Floating inside the KC-135

(somewhere over the Gulf of Mexico)

The Autonomous Shadow

Inside the KC-135 with Colonel Patrick Forrester
U.S. Astronaut and West Point class of 1979

(The team from left to right is, Brock Hershberger, Matt Paretti, Shawn Lough, and myself)

The team before launch

(With Colonel William "Bill" McArthur, U.S. Astronaut and
West Point graduate from the class of 1973)

12

The Hat

As I walked into my room after completing my last West Point examination, I heard my phone ringing. Due to my uncontrollable happiness, I answered the call with pure excitement in my voice.

"This is Cadet Pysh, how may I help you, Sir or Ma'am?"

On the other end of the phone I heard, "Preston, it's Dad. We're here."

After a short conversation on the phone, I told my father that I was on my way to meet them at the North Dock along the Hudson River.

Anytime my family came to visit, my grandparents and parents would travel in a bus motor home and park at the North Dock. The motor coach allowed them to stay on the post for the duration of their stay. It was more convenient than having to stay an hour away in Newburgh, New York. Additionally, it provided my friends and me a safe haven away from the barracks where we could joke and tell stories all night. The North Dock is a beautiful area because it's nestled below the large Hudson cliffs and alongside the river. After hustling my way to the dock, I could tell my parents were just as excited to see me because they met me halfway from the dock.

As our converging paths approached shouting distance, I yelled to my parents, "I'm done!"

After hearing my blunt comment, my dad and mom

were speechless. My father's only plausible reaction was raising his hand in the air and giving me a thumbs up. After two long hugs, they turned around and started walking me back to the North Dock.

After getting back to my grandparents' coach, they began with a barrage of questions pertaining to the last few months. Because I had been so busy with all my finals and the Autonomous Shadow project, I really didn't have much time to talk to them on the phone. My last few months were very hectic, and they were concerned about my well-being. After telling them how well the tests on the Autonomous Shadow went, my dad brought up a subject that I wasn't very fond of talking about.

He said, "So, are you excited to be branching Ordinance Corps?"

In a sarcastic reply, I said, "I'm thrilled, Dad, just thrilled."

He could tell that I wasn't in the mood to discuss the touchy subject. About seven months earlier, my classmates and I had received the branch of service we would be designated upon graduation. We had numerous branches to choose from, and the system was decided based on our class rank. We could choose anything between a tough and rugged life like the infantry, or a more yuppie branch like military intelligence. There were many choices, but the only one I wanted was aviation. From the time I was in high school, all I wanted to be was an attack helicopter pilot.

The reason the question was so difficult for me to hear was because I had actually received an appointment to branch aviation earlier in the year. I already had a slot for flight school, but it was taken away when I didn't pass my physical. Not only was passing a kidney stone two years earlier one of the most painful experiences in my life, the incident took away my chances of becoming a military pilot. I got the dreaded news slightly after Christmas. After my flight slot was pulled, I was re-branched to the Ordinance Corps. When my dad asked me if I was excited about entering the Ordinance Corps, he didn't mention it to upset me. He was just trying to be optimistic as opposed to dwelling on the past.

When I initially found out that I was going to lose my flight slot, I started making phone calls to everyone in the medical community to hopefully get a waiver. Evidently, I needed to get approval from someone at Fort Rucker, Alabama, in order to get the decision overturned. Fort Rucker is the home of Army aviation and where I would have attended flight school. I remember making one last ditch effort to get the decision overturned when I talked to a nurse at Fort Rucker's hospital where my exam was denied. I pleaded and begged with the random woman, but at the end of the conversation, she gave me a generic response.

"I'll talk to some people and see if they can change their decision."

It was the classic conversation where I knew the person on the other end just hung up the phone and rolled her eyes. I had tried every option at my disposal, but in the end, I needed to accept my new branch and move on.

Despite my dad's well-intended question, I avoided the subject and continued talking about any and everything else. They were happy to hear I had finished taking all my finals and felt everything went well. Graduation was only a week away, and despite the classes being complete, there were a lot of loose ends that needed to be taken care of.

During the final week leading up to graduation, my primary objective was getting all my possessions moved out of the barracks and shipped to my first duty station. I procrastinated a little because I didn't have nearly as much stuff as some of my classmates. Instead of spending time packing, I decided to take my parents and grandparents around the school, introducing them to my teachers and meeting my friends. It was an exciting time to see the joy in all my classmates' faces because everyone knew they had made it.

Later that afternoon, I was instructed by one of my friends that the company tactical officer wanted to see me. The company tactical officer (TAC) was a regular Army officer who was ultimately responsible for the company I lived with. After hearing the news from one of my friends, I immediately became nervous. Typically, it wasn't a good sign when the TAC wanted to have a chat. This usually meant a cadet did something wrong or he was about to be reprimanded. The last thing I wanted to do was get in trouble, especially while my family was visiting for graduation. Before leaving my room, I gave my uniform a quick inspection and reported to the TAC's office.

My tactical officer was a man by the name of Captain (CPT) Ponce Espinoza. He was a West Point graduate and member of the soccer team when he was a cadet. For the last three years he had been my mentor and advisor. I had never gotten into trouble with the Captain, so my apprehension to report to his office was higher than normal.

As I walked into his room and reported at the position of attention, CPT Espinoza told me to remain at attention. This was instantly a bad sign. Anytime an officer tells you to remain at attention it's because he's about to discipline you.

As I braced for the punishment, he said, "Cadet Pysh, I always thought you were a great cadet, but during this last week, something happened."

I couldn't believe my ears. What in the world did I do wrong? I had deliberately remained cautious over the last few months because I was so scared of getting into trouble with only months until the end.

CPT Espinoza slowly continued, "Here you were, out

spending your time at NASA and doing all these great things. I was impressed and thought you had your act together. With that said, I found something that you did."

I could almost feel the sense of regret in each of his words. As I watched his movements very closely, I saw him open a drawer in his desk and pull out a piece of paper.

"Do you recognize this slip of paper?" he questioned.

I instantly recognized the writing as my own. I began to read the small note I had written two years earlier.

"If anyone finds this note, please beat your face and contact me at preston.pysh@us.army.mil, Go Hurricanes, Company H3, Preston Pysh, class of 2003."

After reading the message, I poignantly looked up at the Captain and said, "Sir, I apologize. I left that note in the rafter on the fourth floor two years ago. I didn't think it was something that would upset you or anyone who found it."

The Captain quickly responded to my excuse.

"You don't think I know where you put it? I found it with a contractor when we were looking at replacing the fire detectors. I don't know what I should do, considering you're a week from graduation. I've thought about a bunch of different options. The only one that makes sense is you're going to have to change your plans."

After hearing the words come out of his mouth, I couldn't believe my ears. Was he implying that I wouldn't graduate because of this stupid little note? Before I could contemplate the words any further, he continued.

"You're going to have to change your plans of going into the Ordinance Corps. I just got a call through the chain of command and they informed me that Fort Rucker just approved your waiver to go to flight school. Your punishment is to pack up your things and get to Alabama because you're going to be a pilot. How's that sound?"

Without responding, I just shook my head in disbelief. He couldn't be serious. For the last five months I had been soaked with disappointment for losing my flight slot. Now, four days before graduation, I receive the incredible news that I've been reassigned to my dream job. I actually pinched myself because I felt like the situation was a cruel dream my mind had created. Not only did CPT Espinoza pull off one of the greatest pranks, but he also gave me some of the best news I had ever received. I was now being afforded the opportunity to potentially fly attack helicopters.

After a long and unusual pause, I said, "Sir, you can't be serious."

Looking back at me with a huge smile on his face, he replied, "Yes, I'm serious. I don't know what you did, but they've given you your flight slot back."

At this point, I excused myself from the position of attention and went forward to shake CPT Espinoza's hand. I could tell he was equally excited because he knew it was one of my goals.

Once I got back to my room, I pulled the aviation branch insignia out of my drawer. Without any hesitation, I replaced the ordinance emblem on my uniform with the symbol of a propeller blade with wings. I was so proud; this was something I had desired for a very long time. In order to get my amended orders, I needed to travel about a mile down Thayer Road to a building that wasn't co-located with all the other common cadet areas. In an effort to kill two birds with one stone, I gave my father a call and told him I needed a lift to the other side of the post. Without any hesitation, my parents both volunteered to pick me up by the library. They didn't ask why I needed a ride; they just jumped at the chance to spend more quality time with me.

As I waited for their car to arrive beside Patton's statue, I couldn't wait to tell them the wonderful news. I thought about waiting until after graduation, but the sheer excitement of the situation got the best of me. Within a couple minutes, they had pulled their car alongside my position on the road and I climbed in.

After I got into the car, my mom asked, "What's going on? Where do you need to go?"

As I sat down, I acted like it was just another stop for out-processing.

As humdrum a response as I could muster, I said, "Oh, I just need to get my post changed. I'm getting sent to flight school now."

After a subtle pause, my mom and dad both spun around in their seats so fast that they almost broke their necks.

My mom shouted, "WHAT?!"

Even though I told them the great news in a dreary tone, they knew I wasn't joking. I would have never joked about something like that. My mom, looking like she just saw a ghost, questioned further.

"You're going to flight school?"

My dad was still turned around in the driver's seat as the car moved forward. At this point, I started to talk.

"Yes, yes, yes. I'm going to flight school. CPT Espinoza just told me they approved my waiver."

My mom, still in a state of shock, said, "But I thought your waiver was disapproved."

Rolling my eyes a little, I said, "Yes, Mom. It was disapproved, but for some reason it was reconsidered and now I'm going."

As we continued to drive down the road, I told them the whole conversation that the Captain and I had only a few minutes earlier. They could see I was wearing the new aviation crest on my uniform and the sight boggled their minds. The whole event was such a surprise because I never saw it coming. Months earlier I had given up hope that a change in my branch could even take place. I was only a few days away from graduating and I had never seen a Firstie get his branch changed so close to the end.

The week leading up to graduation sped by. It was already the day before graduation and I was standing in the central area getting ready for our final parade. Parades and ceremonies were commonplace at the Academy, but this one was different than the rest. This was going to be our last time to march with the Corps of Cadets. As we stood in the central area between the barracks, many of my classmates were coming by to congratulate me for getting my slot to flight school back. For no particular reason, most of my classmates in the company were going to flight school. It wasn't common to see a majority of a company branch aviation, but for most of the Firsties in Company H-3, we were heading to Fort Rucker, Alabama, for flight training. I felt like I was part of the team once again when I got my flight slot back.

As we heard the chain of command start issuing the orders to fall into formation, I thought back to my first day. I remembered the horrible feeling I got in my stomach when I had two upperclassmen look back at me for a stupid comment about "getting in formation." Even though I felt as small as an ant that day, I felt as big as a skyscraper on the day of the graduation parade.

Over the four years, I had learned so much and my perspective had been changed many times. As the band began to play, we departed the central area and marched through the sally ports and onto the parade field. West Point parades look like Civil War reenactments because 4,000 cadets come on line in 32 organized company formations. The purpose of the parade is to provide a means for the commanding general to inspect the ranks. The tradition started well over a hundred years ago and has never stopped. For this particular parade, our class would be called from within the ranks to march forward and leave the Corps.

Before the start of the parade, I had talked to an alumnus from the class of 1984. He told me it was tradition for the first-class cadets to leave junk around the formation when they marched forward to leave the underclassmen behind. He said it was always funny to look at the parade field at the end of the ceremony because the stands could see all the junk as the cadets marched away. Unfortunately, this tradition had disappeared through the years and none of my friends had ever heard of the idea. After trying to convince some members of my company to partake in the tradition, most weren't interested because they were so scared of getting in trouble with graduation so close. It was funny watching all my classmates on pins and needles for the entire last month. Despite only getting a few close friends to partake in the activity, I still dropped a little piece of paper that read, "Later, suckers," before we marched forward and out of the Corps forever. I'm sure my keeping with tradition would have made the "old grad," Dr. Malobicky, proud.

The day of graduation was a surreal feeling. It was something I had thought about almost every day for four years, so once it finally arrived, it was hard to believe. Like any other day, we started with breakfast formation. Before eating that morning, we held a brief ceremony to promote the underclassmen to their new ranks. It was always an exciting day for the plebes because it was the first time they got to wear rank on their uniform. Everything moved pretty fast, considering the amount of anticipation running rampant.

At the start of the ceremony, all my classmates marched from the barracks up a large hill to Michie Stadium. After arriving at the stadium, we were released into a massive formation to alphabetize ourselves in the same order we would receive our diplomas. After getting organized, we had about an hour of standing around before the ceremony began. It was wonderful seeing all my classmates so happy. Throughout the four years, it was rare to see so many smiling faces.

As I was talking to one of my best friends, I saw a handful of money being passed down the long gray line of cadets. As the stack of money made its way down my row I pulled out my wallet and added a dollar to the pile. I had always heard about this tradition but wasn't sure when it was executed. It is a custom of the graduating class for each member to give the person with the worst class rank a dollar at graduation. The person who collected this wad of $1,000, all paid in $1 increments, was commonly referred to as the goat. Over the years, the school's goats and valedictorians have shared equal success in their military careers. For example, George S. Patton was a goat, whereas Eisenhower was a valedictorian. This was such a funny tradition, so I was more than happy to participate. I didn't know our goat, but I'm sure he turned out to be a great officer.

Before marching into the stadium I had one final tradition to take care of. Looking down at the spot where I was standing, I realized it was almost the same spot where I waited to enter Michie Stadium for my first day at the Academy. As I reminisced about all the fond memories through the years, I reached up and removed my white garrison cap. I looked down at the brass emblem that was centered in the middle of the hat. The school's crest was absolutely gleaming from the amount of time and effort I had put into polishing it to perfection. After looking at my hat, I conducted a quick little comparison of everyone else standing in my row; they all had flawlessly polished crests as well. After four long years, this was the first time I officially recognized that I had made it!

Still holding my cap, I took out some money and pushed it into the flap on the inside cover. In addition to

the money, I also added a small letter I had written earlier that morning. As I got everything setup just the way
I wanted, I heard the command to "fall in." This was our
cue; it was time to march into the stadium and get our
diplomas.

After making our way to the seats positioned on the
home side of the football field, I gave a quick glance into
the stadium seating. I couldn't believe I actually found
where my family was sitting, considering the massive
crowd in attendance. It was interesting seeing the myriad
of people attending the ceremony. There were parents,
Secret Service agents, young children from the local community, politicians, teachers and faculty, news reporters,
and our commencement speaker, Vice President Cheney.

During his speech, he focused on different aspects of
our road ahead. He highlighted the successes our military had gained in Iraq and Afghanistan and also gave our
class accolades for entering the Army in a time of war. As
he started to talk about our uniform, I slowly looked at
the white hat that one of my classmates was wearing.

The Vice President said:

> "Wherever you are posted, wherever your
> career leads you, I trust you will always remem-
> ber how others see the uniform of the United
> States. Your service might take you to the most
> stable place in the quietest of times, but that uni-
> form is a reminder of what assures stability and
> keeps the peace. At other times, your service
> may take you to dangerous places, and there,
> the sight of an American in uniform will bring
> fear to the violent and hope to the oppressed."

As I heard the audience applaud, I thought about all
the hard sacrifices I had made over the last four years in
order to wear that uniform the Vice President spoke of.

I realized the measly sacrifices I made at the Academy were nothing compared to that of the women and men who risked their lives during previous wars. For me, the ceremony provided a nostalgic time to ponder the blood, sweat, and tears of the men and women who paved the way for my family and me.

At the conclusion of the speech, I could sense the spirit of my class was starting to roar. It was time to have our names called so we could go to the front of the stage and receive our diplomas from the Vice President. Something that I was really impressed with during the ceremony was the effort that the faculty made in pronouncing every graduate's name properly. A week before the ceremony, we were required to record the pronunciation of our name so the announcers wouldn't make any mistake during the ceremony. Having heard my own name pronounced as Fish, Psyh (like Psychology), Pssh, Piesh, Peesh, I was relieved to know it would be pronounced properly during such a significant event. (By the way, it's pronounced like Dish, only the "D" is substituted with a "P.") Anyway, it was time for me to finally grasp the slip of paper that proved my completion of the rigorous four years at the institution. As the announcers correctly pronounced my name, I stepped forward and saluted the Vice President and accepted the invaluable diploma. *What a feeling!* My excitement was probably comparable to someone who had just won the lottery; I had earned my reward.

After walking off the stage, I was handed my lieutenant bars from a member of the class of 1953. I was overjoyed to wave the large scrolled diploma in the air in the direction my family was sitting in the stadium. On my way back to my seat I walked past a member of the class of 2001. His name was First Lieutenant John Fernandez and he had recently been injured twenty miles south of Baghdad. As I walked past his location where he sat in a wheelchair, I saluted him and told him how honored I was to have him attend our graduation. I was as proud to salute this hero as I was to receive my diploma.

At the end of the ceremony, there was only one order left for our class to receive. I looked behind our seats and could see hundreds of children anxiously waiting behind the 50-yard line. The chaperons, who were positioned throughout the stadium, allowed them onto the field for the main event. As anticipation built throughout the stadium, our class' First Captain marched to the front of the massive formation and prepared to give the order. As he called the class to attention, the stadium went silent.

Then, in a loud and thunderous proclamation, he said, "Class...dismissed!"

After hearing the order, I grabbed my hat off my head and quickly lowered it beside my knees. After grabbing one last quick and admirable glance at the gleaming crest, I hurled the hat into the air as high as I could throw it.

From the stands, the neat and orderly formation instantly turned to chaos after hearing the announcement. It looked like an organized ant colony that had just been hit with a rock as people and hats erupted everywhere. It felt like only a few seconds before my classmates and I were inundated with children everywhere. After we threw the hats, the chaperons guarding the string barriers allowed the children to break past the 50-yard line and fetch as many hats as they could carry. Since it was bad luck to keep your white garrison cap, I launched it in the air without any hesitation or expectation to see it again.

As the years went by, I often thought about the little girl or boy who swiped my hat that day. I wondered if they looked at it with admiration or as just another trinket for their room. There were a lot of stories behind that hat, but the only tangible information they could have obtained was from the small note I placed inside.

* * *

Four years after graduation, I was a young Captain stationed in South Korea. I had just finished a flight along the De-Militarized Zone (DMZ) as a platoon leader from an Apache Attack Helicopter battalion. After getting back to the office, I decided to check my e-mail before calling it a day. As I read through the long list of new e-mails, one message's subject caught my eye: "Your West Point Hat." After quickly opening the document, I started to read the e-mail from a Colonel who was the commander of the West Point preparation school. In the message, he said his son had caught my hat during my graduation. The Colonel assured me that his boy kept it in a location that sits above everything else in his room. Additionally, he said his son might be interested in trying to attend the Academy someday. As I continued to read the message, the Colonel was curious to know where I was and what I had done since graduation so he could tell his boy. After reading the e-mail, I was overjoyed to know my hat was in good hands and treasured by its new owner. I responded to the Colonel's e-mail and briefly gave him an overview of my time in the Army. At the conclusion of my response, I told the Colonel that if his son does attend the Academy, nothing would make me prouder than to return for his graduation in order to see my hat thrown once again.

After throwing our hats

With Jack Johannes

Receiving my diploma from the Vice President of the United States, Dick Cheney.

After the Graduation Parade

With Captain Espinoza

After the Graduation Parade

With My Parents

Chapter 1: Leaders listen

Chapter 2: Leaders build effective teams

Chapter 3: Leaders are detail-oriented and they speak up

Chapter 4: leaders are truthful at all times

Chapter 5: Leaders are mentally tough

Chapter 6: Leaders are creative

Chapter 7: Leaders take charge and lead by example

Chapter 8: Leaders learn from their mistakes

Chapter 9: Leaders are competitive. They use their foresight to plan and win.

Chapter 10: Leaders are efficient

Chapter 11: Leaders network with people they admire

Chapter 12: Leaders work hard and posses patience

Summary

Throughout this book, it was my intent to focus on the most important leadership principles I had learned while attending West Point. Although the lessons may be short, mastering these twelve skills could take a lifetime. As each skill is equally important, your road to becoming a successful leader will begin with chapter eight's guidance.

Acknowledging your own deficiencies is one of the hardest tasks for a person to do. Without candidly assessing yourself, improvements in your leadership style will never occur. As I personally look at the list to the left, there are numerous deficiencies I still possess. The important part is acknowledging those deficiencies and taking the proper steps to improve those faults.

Now for the moment of truth. Evaluate yourself next to the key points that have been discussed throughout this book. Good luck, there are great subordinates that desire your leadership. When you're afforded the opportunity to lead, always remember to remain calm, collective, and competent.

Recommended Reading

1. Just Listen: Discover the Secret to Getting Through to Absolutely Anyone, by Mark Goulston M.D.

2. The Five Dysfunctions of a Team: A Leadership Fable, by Patrick Lencioni

3. People Skills: How to Assert Yourself, Listen to Others, and Resolve Conflicts, by Robert Bolton

4. Integrity: The Courage to Meet the Demands of Reality, by Dr. Henry Cloud

5. Lone Survivor: The Eyewitness Account of Operation Redwing and the Lost Heroes of SEAL Team 10, by Marcus Luttrell

6. Cracking Creativity: The Secrets of Creative Genius, by Michael Michalko

7. The 21 Irrefutable Laws of Leadership: Follow Them and People Will Follow You, by John C. Maxwell

8. The Littlest Green Beret: On Self-Reliant Leadership, by Jan Rutherford

9. No Substitute for Victory: Lessons in Strategy and Leadership from General Douglas MacArthur, by Donna Kinni

10. The 80/20 Principle: The Secret to Achieving More with Less, by Richard Koch

11. As a Man Thinketh, by James Allen

12. A Message to Garcia, by Elbert Hubbard

Preston has created a leadership and West Point Forum at:

_____

www.prestonpysh.com

_____

Please feel free to visit the site and add to the topics outlined in this book. Your input and feedback will greatly add to the leadership development for all members.

The Author

Captain Preston Pysh has been a military leader since graduating from West Point in 2003 with a degree in Aerospace Engineering.

Upon Graduation, he attended flight school at Fort Rucker, Alabama, where he became rated in the AH-64D Apache Attack Helicopter.

After flight training, Preston was assigned to the 1-2 Attack Aviation Battalion at Camp Eagle, South Korea. While stationed in Korea, he worked as an Attack Platoon Leader, Battalion Adjutant, and Assistant Operations Officer.

Upon completion of his first overseas tour of duty, Preston attended the Military Intelligence Captain's Career Course at Fort Huachuca, Arizona, and was then stationed at Fort Campbell, Kentucky. Once assigned to the 101st Airborne Division, he served as the Aviation Operations Battle Captain in Operation Enduring Freedom IX in Bagram Afghanistan.

Following a successful combat deployment, Preston was then assigned as the A Company, 1-101st AH-64D Apache Attack Helicopter Company Commander during a second year deployment for Operation Enduring Freedom X-XI. Preston's company was directly responsible for the aerial security of the prominent Operation Dragon Strike mission in Kandahar city. His company performed some of the most kinetic enemy strikes during the nation's most intense fighting in Afghanistan.

Preston is married to his lovely wife, Demi, and they proudly raise their two nieces, Kelly and Jenny.

Acknowledgments

Like any achievement in my life, it has never been accomplished without the help of countless family members, friends, and mentors.

First and foremost, I'd like to thank my beloved wife and nieces for their continued support and help in making this project a success. Demi, this book would have never been completed without your help. Thank you!

In the early stages, I would like to thank Master Sergeant Ramon Aquino and Sergeant First Class Russell Spencer for the continued support and critiques. Additionally, I'd like to thank Jon and Stefanie Copple for their assistance on substance and design. Your comments kept the fuel on the fire. I would especially like to thank Mrs. Holly Raus for her countless hours spent editing and proofing the manuscripts. Your efforts are the only reason this book is possible. Last but not least, I'd like to thank my parents, Gwen and Bill Pysh, and my grandparents, Earl and Nancy Mowery, for their continued love and support. You truly are the best parents and grandparents a child could ever have.

I would like to thank Ruth Goodman for her superior professionalism and countless hours proofreading the final manuscript.

Special thanks go to Colonel John McLaughlin (Ret.), Lieutenant Colonel John Hinck, Lieutenant Colonel Hank Taylor, Lieutenant Colonel Scott Hasken, Lieutenant Colonel Ponce Espinoza, Lieutenant Colonel Patrick O'Brien (Ret.), Major Adam Berlew, Major Bernard Harrington, Cameron Gallagher, Bonnie Kovatch, Scott Montoya, Brice Hansen, John David Galindo, Mitch Rosnick, John Morris, Mac Davis, Jack Johannes, Christopher Dean, Todd Cody, Nick Ryan, Dave Moon, Nick Horton, Steve Crews, Matt Paretti, Shawn Lough, Brock Hershberger,

Katrina Cabrera, Michael Donovan, and Stephanie Christenson. Although scores of people have contributed to this book, not all have been named in this section. I apologize in advance for anyone not mentioned. Your contributions are equally appreciated and deserving.

Bibliography

Burton, D. (2008, March 27). 10 Things You Didn't Know About David Petraeus. Retrieved August 6, 2010, from U.S. News and World Report: http://politics.usnews.com/news/national/articles/2008/03/27/10-things-you-didnt-know-about-david-petraeus.html

Garamone, J. (2008, March 1). Head of Joint Chiefs Says Military Must Adopt Wartime Attitude. Retrieved September 6, 2010, from American Forces Press Service: http://thetension.blogspot.com/2008_02_24_archive.html

Gates, R. (2008, April 22). Text of Secretary of Defense Robert Gates' speech at West Point. Retrieved August 6, 2010, from Stars and Stripes: http://www.stripes.com/news/text-of-secretary-of-defense-robert-gates-speech-at-west-point-1.77986

Joseph, S. K. (2004, October 7). Heroes. Retrieved September 6, 2010, from USAREUR Headquarters: http://www.hqusareur.army.mil/heroes/1st_Lt_Christopher_Dean_Silver_Star.pdf

Pappas, M. G. (n.d.). The Cannon Incident. Retrieved October 12, 2008, from Assembly: http://www.aogusma.org/Pubs/Assembly/010708/macarthur.html

Peters, J. T. (1939, June 12). The American Presidency Project. Retrieved August 6, 2010, from http://www.presidency.ucsb.edu/ws/?pid=15767

Reichenberger, D. (2010, September 6). Johnson, Hugh Samuel. Retrieved September 6, 2010, from Oklahoma Historical Society's Encyclopedia of Oklahoma History and Culture: http://digital.library.okstate.edu/encyclopedia/entries/J/JO008.html

Wolfowitz, P. (2001, June 2). Speech. Retrieved September 6, 2010, from United States Department of Defense: http://www.defense.gov/speeches/speech.aspx?speechid=363

Note: The character's names used in the "aircraft taxi" story (chapter six) were changed. Although the student's names were changed, Major Patrick O'Brien's name was not.

Your feedback on the content of this book would be greatly appreciated. Please feel free to use your smartphone and scan the bar code below to review this product.

A final note of thanks to the reader,

When I first thought of the idea to write this book, I wanted it to be unique. For most people that visit West Point, it may seem like chaos and confusion. I'm sure it's hard for an outsider to understand what leadership lessons are being taught. In a way, I wanted the reader to experience the same hectic journey and sense of accomplishment that cadets experience through their four years at the Academy.

This West Point journey was only possible because of people like you - A hard working, tax paying, American citizen. Without your support for the armed forces and opportunities like the United States Military Academy, I would have never learned these invaluable lessons. Thank you for affording me this awesome responsibility and taking the time to read my book.

Sincerely,

Preston Pysh

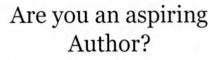

Are you an aspiring Author?

Getting published shouldn't be a dream

Pylon Publishing LLC specializes in the publication of experienced and aspiring authors alike. The small and knowledgeable company can provide the most custom and specialized services necessary to turn your manuscript into a book quickly and effectively. Since Pylon Publishing works directly with the word's largest wholesale book distributor, Ingram Book Company, clients can feel at ease with the widest distribution - Amazon, Barnes and Noble, etc.

It is Pylon Publishing's goal and mission to give authors the most flexibility, distribution, and earnings for their work. As a result, every author retains full control of their book upon publication.

That's the Pylon Promise!

Pylon Publishing LLC

www.pylonpublishing.com